Cause for Hope

Bill Phipps

Cause for Hope

Humanity
at the Crossroads

CopperHouse

Editor: Mike Schwarzentruber
Cover and interior design: Verena Velten
Cover photo: © Björn Kindler/iStochphoto
Pre-Press Production: Chaunda Daigneault
Proofreader: Heather Picotte

CopperHouse is an imprint of Wood Lake Publishing, Inc. Wood Lake Publishing acknowledges the financial support of the Government of Canada, through the Book Publishing Industry Development Program (BPIDP) for its publishing activities. Wood Lake Publishing also acknowledges the financial support of the Province of British Columbia through the Book Publishing Tax Credit.

BNC CERTIFIED | BIBLIOGRAPHIC DATA 2007-08

At Wood Lake Publishing, we practise what we publish, being guided by a concern for fairness, justice, and equal opportunity in all of our relationships with employees and customers. Wood Lake Publishing is an employee-owned company, committed to caring for the environment and all creation. Wood Lake Publishing recycles, reuses, and encourages readers to do the same. Resources are printed on 100% post-consumer recycled paper and more environmentally friendly groundwood papers (newsprint), whenever possible. A percentage of all profit is donated to charitable organizations.

Library and Archives Canada Cataloguing in Publication
Phipps, Bill, 1942-
Cause for hope : humanity at the crossroads / Bill Phipps ; foreword by David C. Korten.
Includes bibliographical references.
ISBN 978-1-55145-555-6
1. Human ecology. 2. Environmental degradation. 3. World politics.
4. Sustainable development. 5. Social justice. 6. Social ethics. I. Title.
GF41.P55 2007   304.2   C2007-903931-6

Published by CopperHouse
An imprint of Wood Lake Publishing Inc.
9590 Jim Bailey Road, Kelowna, BC, Canada, V4V 1R2
www.woodlakebooks.com
250.766.2778

Printing 10 9 8 7 6 5 4 3 2 1
Printed in Canada by Houghton Boston

Dedication

I dedicate this book to my children and their partners:
Sarah and Don; Jeremy and Jodi; Andrea and Blair;
and to my grandchildren Michael and Kate,
the next generation who will inherit our Earthly home.

Table of Contents

Acknowledgments

Those who encouraged me in this project are many. In fact, they include family, friends, colleagues, and mentors, who have taught, supported, pushed, cared for, and loved me throughout my life. I have been blessed beyond measure at each stage of my winding, privileged journey. In only mentioning those who had a direct influence in the writing of this book, I know I will leave out some important people. I tend to consult a lot. I test out ideas, perceptions, analysis, faith, action alternatives. Therefore, a multitude of people have been involved, whether or not they know it, in the writing of this book. Many of them are authors whose works appear in the bibliography.

Among those who have shared in this project are Jim Streeter, David Swann, Raffi Cavoukian, Hal Llewelyn, Christopher Lind, Charles Pascal and the Atkinson Charitable Foundation, Julie Hrdlicka, Judy Chapman, Bob Anderson, Hannah Anderson, Kevin Thomas, Brian Pincott, Barb Kinney, Faith and the Common Good networks, Banff Men's Conference participants, Professional Association of Canadian Theatres, Sierra Club of Canada, Pages Books in Calgary, many individuals and committees of the United Church of Canada, and various interfaith networks. The congregation of Scarboro United Church in Calgary deserves special mention. They have been extremely supportive of all my "outside" endeavors, from my time as Moderator to the writing of this book. I thank the many people who were part of shaping ideas and understand the time "away."

Others have been involved in the more sustained or detailed way. David and Fran Korten opened their home, minds and hearts at the early stages of my thinking about the book. John Minear and Nancy Maxson provided wonderful space and keen insight. My sister Elda Thomas gave me the unrestricted use of her cottage south of Minden, Ontario from where our grandparents came and near which I attended Kilcoo Camp as a teenager. Her generosity was a great gift. Roger and Moira Hutchison hosted a lively dinner and conversation at their home with Ted Reeve, Katharine Vansittart, David Fallis, Walter and Ida Pitman, Stephen Scharper. King's Fold Retreat Centre near Cochrane,

Alberta provided a perfect writing venue overlooking the tranquility of the Ghost River.

George Melnyk provided the initial confidence, idea and encouragement to seriously begin work on this book. Graciously he steered me away from pitfalls and into a more productive approach. Wood Lake Publishing shared enough confidence and interest to actually offer a contract. I would especially like to thank my editor, Mike Schwartzentruber, who was enthusiastic from the beginning and who guided me through the process with great care.

Of course none of this would have been possible without the encouragement, ideas, confidence and sustaining love of Carolyn Pogue, wife and companion in our amazing journey together. She typed every word and believed in my capacity to see this through despite all my doubts.

So I thank deeply all of the people mentioned and others who believed along the way that these ideas and stories needed to be told.

Foreword
Change the Story, Change the Future
David C. Korten

Some years ago, Thomas Berry wrote in *Dream of the Earth* that we humans need a new story. It was a prophetic insight that set forth a defining challenge for many who read his inspiring treatise. The Very Reverend Bill Phipps was among them, and this book is his response to that challenge.

As Reverend Phipps notes, we humans live by the stories that define our cultural beliefs and values. This simple insight is a key to understanding why, for some 5,000 years, humans have accepted systems of imperial rule in which men rule over women, the light skinned rule over the dark sinned, the psychologically dysfunctional rule over the psychologically mature, and the majority of humans are condemned to lives of exclusion and deprivation.

For five millennia, those who enjoy the privileges of power have legitimated their rule by stories that celebrate their special virtue, dismiss the oppressed as inferior beings unworthy of respect, and affirm the division between the privileged and the excluded as a proper and inevitable response to the human condition. In our time, these stories include religion stories that tell us that nothing happens except by the will of God, therefore we must accept the existing division of wealth and power as a manifestation of God's will. They also include science stories of Darwinian evolution that tell us progress depends on a brutal competition, in which those most fit win and rightfully prosper as the unworthy lose and rightfully perish.

These and other defining stories of our culture induce a kind of cultural trance that legitimates a self-destructive dominator system, resulting in suppression of the creative potential of all but the most favoured members of our species. Our future depends on breaking the trance through a cultural and spiritual awakening.

In *Cause for Hope*, Reverend Phipps tells of his personal awakening to the arrogance and injustice legitimated by old stories he was taught to accept as a youth, and of how he came to question and ultimately challenge these stories publicly in his adult role as one of Canada's most prominent civic and religious leaders. In sharing the story of his personal path from innocence to awakening, Reverend Phipps gives us permission to question the stories we learned in our youth, publicly discuss our doubts, and join with others to consider new possibilities.

To maintain the power of the trance that holds us captive to a dominator system, Empire depends on our silence and isolation. Cecile Andrews, author of *The Circle of Simplicity*, gives an example from the women's movement, which has largely changed the prevailing cultural story on gender. Much of the early work of the women's movement centred on women forming conversation groups in which they came together to share their personal stories. Prior to these conversations, the prevailing gender story taught that the key to a woman's happiness is to find the right man, marry him, and devote her life to his service. Women whose lives did not conform to this story were taught that this was a sign of their personal failing. Rather than reveal their "deficiency," most remained silent and thus isolated. When women began coming together to share their stories, they learned the truth that this story worked for few women, if any, suggesting that the fault was not with themselves, but rather with a false story. By breaking their silence, they ended their isolation and initiated a collective search for a new story that is now playing out in a continuing revolution in gender relations.

Andrews has participated in carrying forward the same process in the voluntary simplicity movement. Corporate advertisers bombard us with the story that material goods are our measure of self-worth and the pathway to happiness. We are expected to believe that unless we express a passion to shop and consume, we are out of step, unworthy of love, perhaps even unpatriotic for posing a threat to the economic prosperity of the nation.

The success of the voluntary simplicity movement centres on bringing people together in conversation circles in which they share their stories of what actually brings them pleasure in life. By this simple act, the silence is broken, the isolation is ended, and people find the courage to begin publicly living a new story of material sufficiency rich in the joys of family and community life. Liberated from the trance of consumerism, living their new story, and demonstrating a more fulfilling way of living, they inspire the liberation of others. It is a powerful sequence. Break the silence. End the isolation. Change the story. Change the human course.

I've experienced the power of this sequence through my personal involvement in mobilizing the global opposition to corporate globalization. When I was serving as a member of the foreign aid establishment in Asia, I gradually became aware that there was something odd about the constantly repeated economic development story being told with great emphasis by the World Bank, the International Monetary Fund (IMF), other official aid agencies, and most mainstream economists. According to this story, the key to development success, universal prosperity, and the end of poverty is to deregulate markets, eliminate trade barriers, privatize public assets and services, finance development with foreign borrowing, eliminate restrictions on foreign ownership of domestic assets, keep labour cheap, and orient the domestic economy to production for export.

Although the proponents would not put it in these terms, the official story essentially says that the more your economy is controlled by foreign interests and managed for their benefit, the faster it will grow and thus the better off you will be. Although this is utter nonsense on its face, the story had such strong support from credentialed experts that few people were willing to challenge it.

Throughout the 1980s, the World Bank and the IMF used the story to impose draconian policy "reforms" on deeply indebted nations as a precondition to receiving new loans to refinance previous loans to avoid total economic collapse. They called it Structural Adjustment. The result was ever deeper indebtedness, foreign dependence, and poverty. Anyone who dared to challenge this story was ridiculed, dismissed as ill-informed, or reviled as mean-spirited for attacking policies essential to lifting the poor out of their misery. Yet it is self-evident to anyone who takes the time to think it through that the official story has nothing to do with helping the poor and everything to do with increasing the economic power and profits of some very large and rapacious corporations. It is the old colonialism clad in new robes.

In the late 1980s, I became one of the few credentialed voices who dared issue a public challenge to this perverse story. I joined with other critics, as I found them, to form a rag-tag alliance devoted to speaking truth to whomever was willing to listen. We had few resources beyond our volunteer energy, and our critiques circulated only through small obscure networks largely unknown beyond their own members. Yet each voice that broke the silence gave courage to others. Within a few years, millions of people all around the world were calling for action to stop the devastation caused by neo-liberal development policies, and were mobilizing massive demonstrations that undermined the destructive work and eroded the public legitimacy of both the World Bank and the IMF.

Even within the small initial group of critics, I was among the first to call for closing the World Bank and the IMF as inherently destructive institutions with no beneficial role – a call almost universally dismissed at the time as an unrealistic fantasy. The idea that these institutions may one day be decommissioned now seems a real possibility.

In the early 1990s, the forces of corporate rule turned to international trade agreements as their primary instrument for advancing what insiders referred to as the Washington Consensus – the reigning ideology of the World Bank, the IMF, and the U.S. Treasury Department, an institutional triumvirate located in Washington, D.C., devoted to advancing the interests of Wall Street financiers. According to the official story, freeing markets and trade from unwarranted interference by self-serving government bureaucracies unleashes a powerful engine of economic growth that brings prosperity, opportunity, democracy, and peace to all people, and generates the wealth needed to end poverty and heal the environment.

Resistance against this expanded assault on democracy and on the public interest under the guise of trade agreements began with a tiny network of Asian citizen activists centred in Penang, Malaysia. Their efforts awakened others, leading to a small international gathering in San Francisco in 1994, at which some 45 citizen activists from around the world shared their stories of how this assault was playing out in each of the countries and regions in which they lived. From these presentations, a picture quickly emerged of a well-organized assault by powerful transnational corporations on people, nature, and the institutions of democracy in the cause of increasing corporate profits.

I had the privilege of being a part of this initial gathering, which led to the formation of the International Forum on Globalization (IFG). Through the IFG, we developed and projected our analysis out into the world, through teach-ins, reports, and books; and through the speaking, writing, and networking outreach of our individual members and their organizations. My book *When Corporations Rule the World* was part of this effort.

As the new story spread, it unleashed a powerful global citizen's movement supported by an ever growing network of people, numbering in the millions. The massive demonstrations that forced an early closure of the World Trade Organization meeting held in Seattle in 1999 thrust this movement into the public consciousness. The word was out that far from ending poverty, saving the environment, and spreading peace and freedom, the structural adjustment policies of the IMF and the World Bank, and the "free" trade agreements of the World Trade Organization were spreading social and environmental exploitation, stripping democratic governments of their power to serve the public good, and fuelling violence.

From 1999 forward, wherever the corporate elites met to advance their imperial agenda, they were greeted by massive demonstrations in defence of economic justice, peace, the environment, and democracy. Within a few years, this movement gained significant global media attention, largely stalled the corporate-led free-trade juggernaut, and established global civil society as a potent political force. Thus was born from the most humble of beginnings, one of the most powerful, international, and inclusive social movements of the human experience. Recognizing that resistance alone is a losing strategy, people everywhere were soon countering the elitist program of corporate-led economic globalization with programs of community-led economic localization. It all happened within a span of little more than ten years.

These and other struggles for justice, peace, and democracy are far from complete, but what has been accomplished provides ample evidence that changing the stories that frame the public discourse, even those promoted by powerful interests, is possible. Indeed, challenging stories fabricated to serve systems of domination may be the most powerful social change intervention that small groups of citizens can undertake, because it is a struggle in which truth ultimately holds the edge. Change a defining story and the society eventually changes its course.

The most basic of our stories are those by which we understand our human origins, our human nature, and our human relationship to one another, Earth, and creation. These stories are the source of our deepest spiritual/religious beliefs. Indeed, they are generally so central to our being that there is a tendency to dismiss any suggestion that they be subject to critical examination as an act of sacrilege.

Yet, as Reverend Phipps explains, many of our most widely-believed and recited stories, including many of our religious stories, have been altered or even fabricated to serve the political interests of a corrupt and destructive system at odds with the deeper spiritual wisdom on which each of the world's great religious traditions was originally founded. As he observes, in many instances, the stories of indigenous peoples, which modern imperial cultures have ridiculed and sought to wipe out, are grounded in an understanding of our sacred connection to Earth and creation that we must now as a species reclaim – drawing from the wisdom of all the world's many peoples and cultures.

This is the work before us and *Cause for Hope* is an essential guidebook.

Preface

This book seeks to achieve a number of objectives. First, I believe that the faith traditions of the world are called to respond to the growing challenges facing our Earthly home. There is little doubt that the planet we all share is sick and in grave danger. Although political, economic, and social factors have all contributed to the Earth's condition, spiritual questions lie at the heart of the crisis we face. I believe faith communities need to step forward and give leadership.

One way of interpreting the crisis we face is through the lens of the narratives we live. By contrasting the "Old Story," which has shaped and defined Western culture and which has brought us to our current situation, with a possible "New Story," we can begin to understand how the global community can move from destructive paralysis to life-giving transformation. Reverence for the Earth, with all its complex mystery and abundance, will help us work together toward the good of ecological integrity, respect, and dignity. Writing and living a New Story will help us get there.

Second, I believe that we can no longer treat major issues in isolation from one another. Everything is connected, interrelated. Actions in one field of concern have consequences for other realities. Yet, quite often, we are unaware of the ripple effects of our actions, because we remain focused on just one or two issues. Economic justice, peace building, gender equality, disease, racial respect, ecological integrity, scientific knowledge – just to name a few – are all intimately connected and interrelated. The obscene gap in living conditions, including consumption, between rich and poor; the prevalence of diseases such as malaria and HIV/ AIDS; debasing patriarchy and ecological destruction: all of these things need to be treated together, as a whole. No longer can we afford to have environmentalists and social justice advocates competing with each other, or worse, regarding each other with suspicious skepticism.

Third, I believe that faith traditions need to emerge from behind doctrinal and theological differences to work together for the common good. In many ways their social ethics complement each other, leading us all to common ground. Thankfully, both global and local movements exist for interfaith dialogue and action. However, these efforts need to intensify and coalesce around the common goal of addressing the unprecedented challenges humankind and the Earth face. Spiritual wisdom and leadership is essential.

The main body of this book seeks to address these concerns. I have also included an extensive Appendix of related material, containing statements and interviews in which people have expressed keen interest. In particular, I have included material surrounding "the controversy" resulting from my interview with the *Ottawa Citizen* newspaper shortly after my election to the position of Moderator of the United Church of Canada. I have also included apologies to First Nations peoples, and speeches relating to issues I raise in the body of the book.

The book also contains an extensive if partial bibliography. Many of the authors represented there have become trusted friends in understanding our wondrous world and how we may live within its embrace with respect, dignity, justice, and peace – that is, with love.

Lastly, I provide discussion questions at the end of each chapter in the hope that people may engage these issues together in lively conversation. There are many treatments of the concerns I raise that are scholarly, in greater depth, and more focused. My goal is to raise both the alarm and the cause for hope in an accessible and timely way.

Prologue

Once there was a beautiful, clear, sparkling spring that served the needs of a mid-sized village. People revered this source of life. People relied on it, rejoiced in it, and protected it from all harm. This natural gift of creation had sustained the village since before memory.

One day, some leaders decided that the village should honour the spring as a sacred place. They discussed what to do and finally decided to erect a building beside it so that strangers would know the spring's significance. They built a little shrine, with a simple altar, and a candle that always burned with a warm, reassuring glow.

Over the generations, the villagers added to the shrine. They enlarged the shrine so that people could hold periodic religious services. They built other rooms on to the shrine so that people could sit and meditate. They put in a paved walkway so that people could easily get to the shrine. Over time, the spring became invisible. It was covered by this huge building. The fresh water still flowed, but people had to go inside to a tap in the corner of the building. Each generation of people, it seemed, wanted to make the site bigger and more beautiful. It eventually became a cathedral.

After still more years passed, technology improved. People discovered that they could pipe their water from a large, distant lake directly into their own homes. They no longer had to go to the cathedral. The tap in the corner of the cathedral was turned off and replaced by a small shrine to water.

More years passed, and the cathedral grew in importance as a gathering place. Religious leaders held special ceremonies. Still more additions were built on to the great edifice. The fresh crystalline water from the underground spring became a memory, the story of its existence a tale told once each year on a special religious holiday.

The village had also grown into a modern city, with expressways, malls, traffic, and big-box stores, in addition to the struggling yet attractive and historical downtown core. Industrial development had grown up on the outskirts of the city. Despite modest efforts at prevention, and despite modern technology, which removed many of the remaining toxins, the waste from industrial production seeped into the soil. As a result, the drinking water for the city, now piped from the underground aquifers, became compromised. Because the piped water was no longer of good quality, people purchased bottled water from far off places. It was expensive.

Of course, conflicts arose over water prices and other issues of power, and over whose ritual should prevail at the cathedral.

And so a day arrived when not only grand edifices covered springs of living water, but dogmas, ideology, and national and religious pride divided people from each other, from the Earth, and from the creative divine energy, which gives life itself.

The original story of the shared, life-giving spring had slowly disappeared. In its place another story arose. This story was all about control, domination, conflict, self-righteousness, arrogance, growing disparity in wealth and power, fear, extreme individualism, greed, cynicism, and a host of other disrespectful characteristics, which divided all life into complex categories of greater and lesser.

One day, a young person from far away came to the city, having heard stories of a mysterious life-giving spring of water located somewhere under a magnificent cathedral. Now, it should be noted that few people attended the ceremonies at the cathedral anymore. They were so overtaken with the current story (of alienation from just about everything), that few remembered the ancient story at all.

The young person had studied and had learned everything she could about water. She had learned about various forms of pollution, and about the resistance of governments, industry, and farmers to acknowledge the dangers to water. She also had studied ancient rituals concerning water; she knew it was essential for life on Earth and therefore understood its deeply spiritual significance. She had become involved with activist organizations seeking to change attitudes and to enact public policy to recognize water as a human right to be protected.

So the young person started asking questions about the ancient story of the spring and about the current ways of living, which appeared so destructive and self-defeating. She proposed the possibility of learning a new story, whose characteristics were peace, harmony, dignity, respect, and the honouring of children and elders, the Earth and all its creatures.

However sensible her inquiries may have been, she met resistance. After all, life in the city was comfortable. People knew and cherished their rituals, ceremonies, and practices. Why change? Why ask all these questions? Why move from familiar ways of being and doing to new, untested ways?

The people dismissed the young woman as being... well... young. And inexperienced. Yes, some of the concerns she raised were legitimate, but solutions would be found. Somewhere. Somehow. New technologies would be developed, eventually. More time and money were needed, that was all. There was no need for radical evaluation, or for wild actions. They just had to be patient.

But the young woman would not give up. She talked with individuals, met with small groups, wrote articles for the newspaper, and tapped into the growing concerns of like-minded people, even though they were a minority. Soon more people began to recognize the wisdom of her questions and the sincerity of her passion. One by one, they joined her cause. Bit by bit, step by step, letter by letter, things began to change. Conversations, debates and eventually even public demonstrations took place.

Eventually, the young woman persuaded the citizens to tear down the cathedral and to locate the spring of crystalline water. Next, she persuaded them to question their dogmas, ideologies, and conventions, which had prevented a new story from being born.

But she didn't stop there. She persuaded people from all religious traditions and ideologies to gather in a circle around the spring of water, to tell their own stories without interruption. The only rules were that everyone had to truly listen to the others when they talked, and that no one could try to persuade the others about the exclusive truth of their particular experience, story, or belief. The young woman believed that each tradition contained truth and was part of a larger story of the universe in which all creation lived. She also believed that for life to continue on Earth in any meaningful way, all people – with their own particular stories about the mystery of life – needed to respect each other and to work together for the common good of all creatures and of the Earth itself. By gathering around the spring in a circle, in which no one dominated, they would honour the spring as a symbol of their shared humanity, their occupying common ground for the common good. Through such patient sharing and commitment, the Earth would be restored, peaceful harmony would be realized, and laughter would again echo throughout the valley.

The people agreed to her proposal and began meeting together. We don't know the outcome yet. The process is just beginning. But there are signs that give us hope that a new story is being born, a story that is an integral part of the larger story being told by the universe itself. Indeed, we are all being invited to give birth to such a story wherever we are. Only then will the Earth and its creatures have a future.

I. Crossroads

Global society stands at a crossroads, one of those critical moments in the history of humankind. The simple fact is that Earth cannot support the rampant overuse and misuse of its abundant gift of resources. Not only are we depleting the forests, oceans, soil, and water, we are also poisoning the air and polluting our rivers, lakes, and oceans. We are living far beyond our means. Life as we are creating it is measurably and extravagantly unsustainable.

I live in oil-rich Calgary, one of the most prosperous places on Earth. Ignoring experience all over North America, we seem intent on repeating the mindlessly unsustainable and ugly urban sprawl that plagues this continent. We are paving our way to Montana and to the Rockies with total disregard to sustainability. Urban sprawl and our dependence on cheap oil, which has almost run out, are just two examples of why and how humanity finds itself at a crossroads.

Other examples include extreme consumerism, the growing gap between rich and poor, frightening pandemics such as HIV/AIDS, the continuing development of nuclear weapons, wasteful energy choices, and violence in all forms. All of these things threaten the very future of our children. However daunting each of these issues is by itself, we now know that everything is interconnected. As human beings, we depend upon clean air and water, upon freedom from violence and disease; we depend upon the intricate balance of the Earth's ecosystems, and upon each other. We can no longer separate spheres of human activity. Our politics, economics, education, and religion, among other things, are interwoven in ways we have forgotten.

Not only that, but, taken as a whole, this crossroads we face is a spiritual issue of the deepest order. The fundamental questions we face are spiritual. What are human beings for? Or as Peter Short, former moderator of the United Church, says, "What are humans being for?" How do we relate to the Earth and to all living creatures, including each other? Yes, these are political, economic, social, cultural, and religious issues. But at their core and threading them all together are profound spiritual questions.

The times are daunting indeed. These are scary, bewildering days. Too much is coming at us too fast. We are inundated by too much information. The Internet gives us anything we want; reliability and trustworthiness are another matter. It is all too overwhelming for most, so "let us just go shopping," as George W. Bush encouraged after September 11, 2001. We might as well live as highly and as extravagantly as possible, because these challenges are too complicated and, anyway, maybe all those Nobel-prize winning people are wrong. Except that they're not wrong. We've already begun to experience the effects of climate change, for example, and it will hit our children even harder than it has hit us. And our grandchildren? What kind of world will they inhabit? Based on what we've seen and experienced already, it's a safe bet it won't be pretty.

There is another approach, of course, and people of all nationalities and from all walks of life, and from all disciplines, classes, races, and religions are taking it up. Recognizing and celebrating the interdependence of all life, and the common spiritual thread that runs through this beautiful fabric, people are taking up the challenge of facing the crossroads and are turning in a different direction. Many of these people are ridiculed, marginalized, or otherwise ignored. But this global awakening will not be put down. Celebrating common spiritualities and shared worldviews, these people and movements are discerning the times and are acting accordingly.

Two such people are David Korten and Raffi Cavoukian. Korten's book *The Great Turning: From Empire to Earth Community* calls for a social transformation that will lead to a sustainable future. Korten understands how everything is connected. He is not embarrassed to speak in the same breath about economics, politics, ecology, and spirituality. While recognizing that we stand at a crossroads, he gives us a way forward that is both positive and possible.

Just as timely is Raffi Cavoukian's *Child Honoring: How to Turn this World Around*. Like Korten, he understands that we inhabit a momentous time in history, and he invites us to look at the global crisis through the lens of "child honouring." How does what we do affect children? When we look at economic decisions, political practices, ecological neglect, and every other human activity through the lens of child honouring, a clarity of purpose and action emerges. The concept of child honouring provides an organizing principle around which we can create a culture of peace and sustainability. (I have included Cavoukian's "Covenant for Honouring Children" in Appendix B.)

Cavoukian's and Korten's contributions complement each other. They provide inspiration to those of us bewildered as to what to think, feel, and do. Their ideas are specific. Along with others, they give us hope.

In fact, crossroads moments are times of exciting and surprising spiritual discernment. They are moments in history when the divine energy, the creative impulse at the heart of life, reveals itself – enlightening us, challenging us, and loving us into being and action.

It should be clear from the above that I do not believe our time is unique; this is not the first crossroads humanity has ever faced. At the same time, I am not an alarmist, one who constantly says that everything is falling apart. Nor do I believe in conspiracy theories. On the contrary, I believe that people and large institutions can change, that they can and often do learn to do things differently.

Ray Anderson and his company, Interface Incorporated, stand as a perfect example of this. Anderson founded Interface in the early 1980s. Since then it has grown to become the largest manufacturer of commercial and modular carpet in the world. A public company, Interface does business in more than 100 countries, and has sales of close to one billion dollars.

Carpet-making is a petro-intensive industry, involving extensive use of chemicals and energy. Traditionally, it uses a great deal of water, and generates enormous amounts of waste, greenhouse gases, effluent, and scrap material. When Mr. Anderson became fully aware of how polluting and unsustainable his manufacturing processes were, he resolved to take action. Since 1994, Interface has been on a mission called "climbing Mount Sustainability."

Whereas once it might have been guilty of plundering the Earth, Interface now does everything possible to preserve the Earth. For example, to date, it has reduced its water consumption by 66 percent. Its net greenhouse gas emissions are down 52 percent. It has reduced waste by close to

50 per cent, and it sends 80 percent less scrap to the landfill. Interface's goal is to achieve a zero ecological footprint by 2020. This will require a closed-loop manufacturing process, in which everything is recycled or used up in the manufacturing process itself. It will produce no waste or pollution.[1]

Ray Anderson faced his own personal crossroads, rose to the challenge, and took the path of sustainability. If such a large and complex industrial company can turn itself around with such passionate resolve, why not others?

Yet we cannot deny that we live in dangerous times. Some refer to our age as the sixth great extinction, the previous one having occurred 65 million years ago when the dinosaurs disappeared. The death march across our Earth is unprecedented in human history. Half the world's forests have been cut down and the rest are under constant threat. The oceans are being "fished out" at an alarming rate.

We are learning how disastrous large-scale, industrial, chemically dependent farming has become. Not only is the soil being impoverished, so are the rural communities from Canada to China who depend upon it.

As if that weren't enough, it takes three calories of fossil fuel energy to produce one calorie of food. Even more ridiculous is the fact that it takes 10 or more calories of fuel to get that food to our tables.[2]

In *The Long Emergency*, James Howard Kunstler argues compellingly that we are near the end of the oil-based economy, which was really a small and wasteful (if extremely productive and innovative) blip on the tides of history. From the curiously ridiculous distances food travels around the world, to airline travel, to sprawling suburbia, to just about anything North Americans take for granted, all of it is about to collapse.

In my home province of Alberta, we spend billions of dollars to extract dirty oil from the tar sands, at tremendous cost to the ecological integrity of the area, and to First Nations viability and culture (never considered when calculating the "cost" of the product itself), only to fuel the wasteful American military-industrial complex. A few people are becoming exceedingly rich, but at what cost to just about everything else?

The crossroads we face is daunting indeed. Wendell Berry, American farmer, philosopher, and environmentalist, puts this challenge to us: "We have lived by the assumption that what was good for us was good for the world. We have been wrong. We must change our lives so that it will be possible to live by the contrary assumption that what is good for the world will be good for us."

Thomas Berry, in his book *The Great Work*, calls such crossroads times "moments of grace." Indeed, these are exciting days, because we can make choices. These are days of privilege, because we can rise to the challenge and declare our true beliefs; we can understand our deep spiritual yearnings, and connect the dots of what we say we believe to the dots of how we actually live. If we are open to the Spirit hovering over and within our lives, we can experience the current crossroads as a moment of grace, gently nudging us to a "great transformation."

Amazing things can happen when we discern the signs of the times as holy conversation; when we discern them as grace spaces in which the cosmic divine energy speaks to us, just as it did with Isaiah, Jeremiah, Esther, Mary, Jesus, and countless prophets and elders of all traditions. These crossroads present us with opportunities to learn who we are in this great planetary enterprise, where we belong in the vast web of life that shares our Earthly home, and how we can express the very best in human nature.

Millions of individuals and innumerable organizations around the world are building bridges across seemingly intractable barriers, thereby overcoming the narrow mentalities and shallow vision that have put us in such peril in the first place.

An important example for me is Women in Black. With groups in more than 40 countries, Women in Black regularly stand vigil in city squares, silently pleading for a non-violent world. As well as in Calgary and in New York City, I have stood with them in Jerusalem, where they began in 1988 as a witness to non-violent action in the Israeli-Palestinian struggle. The women come from different faith traditions (and some from no faith tradition), and believe fervently in the unity of the human family. As a worldwide movement, they represent one of the thousands of global initiatives the media routinely ignore. Our political, corporate, and media leaders would rather inculcate fear than promote hope.

Still, movements and organizations all over the globe are rising up to challenge the big boys with narrow and arrogant minds, who flaunt international law, who see resources as theirs for the taking, and who show so little respect for people and for the Earth. The people and groups to which

I refer stand as proof that each life matters and that each of us can make a difference. It is our choice. We have the material, mental, and spiritual resources to live these moments of grace with hope, and for the sake of transformation.

In *Ancient Futures: Learning from Ladakh*, Helena Norberg-Hodge says the following:

> Western society today is moving in two distinct and opposing directions. On the one hand, mainstream culture led by government and industry moves relentlessly toward continued economic growth and technological development, straining the limits of nature and all but ignoring fundamental human needs. On the other hand, a counter-current, comprising a wide range of groups and ideas, has kept alive the ancient understanding that all life is inextricably connected.[3]

I am conscious of having to make choices every time I go grocery shopping, use the car, travel by plane, run for political office, preach a sermon, buy gifts. Often I feel guilty or conflicted, but I am becoming more aware of how co-opted, embedded, or bribed I am by our hyper-consumer culture.

No choice is without consequence. The trick is not to feel paralyzed, depressed, or too guilty. In fact, maintaining a healthy sense of humour and perspective goes a long way to helping us live responsibly. Healthy scepticism, sprinkled with a developing social conscience, helps us open our eyes and hearts to alternative ways of being in the world. As someone who hates change, I find myself risking more Earth-friendly and just decisions.

I close this chapter with a prayer from Arthur Solomon, an Ojibway elder. I met him once at a gathering of people seeking to find ways to heal the enormous chasm between First Nations and non-Native people. He was one of those marvellous elders who sought courageously to bring people together.

Grandfather,

Look at our brokenness.

We know that in all Creation

Only the human family

Has strayed from the Sacred Way.

We know that we are the ones

Who are divided

And we are the ones

Who must come back together

To walk in the Sacred Way.

Grandfather,

Sacred One,

Teach us love, compassion, and honour

That we may heal the Earth

And heal each other.[4]

Discussion Questions

1. Do you believe that global society is at a major cross-roads?

2. If your answer is no, explain your reason. How would you characterize this point in history?

3. If your answer is yes, what do you think are the distinguishing marks of this crossroads?

4. What gifts, resources, and beliefs help you face this crossroads?

5. How does this moment in history affect your decision-making (compared, for example, to the last decade)?

---

1. To learn the full story, see Ray Anderson's book *Mid-Course Correction: Toward a Sustainable Enterprise: The Interface Model* (Atlanta: The Peregrinzilla Press, 1999). Also see Ray Anderson's chapter in Raffi Cavoukian and Sharna Olfman's book, *Child Honoring: How to Turn this World Around* (Westport, CT: Praeger, 2006).

2. Carl N. McDaniel, *Wisdom for a Livable Planet* (San Antonio: Trinity University Press, 2005), 106.

3. As quoted in McDaniel, *Livable Planet*, 83.

4. Arthur Solomon, *Songs for the People: Teachings on the Natural Way* (Toronto: NC Press Ltd., 1990), 159.

2. The Importance of Story

All societies live by their stories, narratives, or myths. These stories reflect who we are and determine who we will be. Rooted in tradition, they convey and define our roles, priorities, and values; and provide a vision of who we can become. Both consciously and sub-consciously, our stories shape who we are as we reflect them in the social, political, and economic structures we create. We make personal and political decisions within the context of our society's overarching narrative. Our economic and ethical choices both reflect and shape the underlying narrative we live out individually and collectively.

Individualistic narratives

If the narrative by which we live emphasizes individualism, personal gain, a win-at-all-costs mentality, exclusivity, power over, and other related characteristics, the society we create will reflect these elements in its shape, structures, and ways of being and doing. Public policy will emphasize individual initiative and responsibility, and will minimize collective and cooperative responsibilities. People will need to "fend for themselves." There will be no limit to the wealth individuals can accumulate, nor to the poverty into which people can sink. Privatization of public services will become desirable (to some). Government funding for public enterprise will give way to increasing reliance on lotteries, on state-sponsored-and-encouraged gambling, and on private fundraising. A society of winners and losers will quickly develop and be celebrated. Moral judgements will be made against those who are unable to compete. Mean-spiritedness will creep into public discourse and leadership.

As a result, feelings of fear become pervasive on all levels. Fear creates separation – more gated communities, more security systems, and more private police forces. Fear creates suspicion, mistrust, and more aggressive behaviour.

Fear creates an economy of scarcity, and therefore of accumulation, in which people strive to get and to keep wealth as quickly and as vigorously as possible before someone else gets it or it disappears altogether.

This type of narrative undermines communal institutions and networks of collective rights and responsibilities. The planet becomes a battleground, where competing interests determine who will win and who will lose, who will have power and who will be marginalized.

Communal narratives

On the other hand, if the narrative we live emphasizes community, collective well-being, a desire for everyone to win, inclusivity, power with, and related characteristics, these elements will determine the shape of the society we create, and the ways in which it functions. Public policy will emphasize collective and communal responsibility. It will encourage individual initiatives within a framework of collective action and collective well-being. People will feel supported and encouraged by publicly funded institutions. There will be no limit to the good of inclusivity. Everyone will participate in raising the standards of individual and communal well-being. Efforts will be made to ensure that no one lives in poverty, receives a sub-standard education, or is left out of prosperity. Governments will not rely on the evils of gambling, or on the whim of private donations.

Rather than fear, trust develops and grows. A sense of belonging – to each other, to the local community, and to the Earth itself – takes root. Individuals come to know that they are valued as part of the human family and as part of the Earth community. Communal institutions and networks of rights and responsibilities are enhanced. Rather than a battleground, the planet becomes a home in which all feel secure and valued.

When narratives collide

The influence and importance of societal or cultural narratives becomes especially clear when differing narratives collide. Historically, for example, First Nations societies have been governed by a different story than Western industrial societies. I believe that a root cause of the chasm and antagonism between First Nations and European capitalist/missionary societies is the totally different narratives through and under which they live.

When European peoples came to the North American continent, they brought with them their governing narratives and cultural values, which included attitudes of superiority. They forced aboriginal peoples to abandon their stories, which they ridiculed and even outlawed. In this way, aboriginal peoples were exiled from their guiding story, the very thing that gave their lives meaning. Many have been wandering aimlessly ever since, while others have had to struggle long and hard to remember their stories and to keep them alive.

Through a variety of experiences, I am coming to understand just how deeply the experience of colonialism, indeed of cultural genocide, has affected the First Peoples of Canada. In fact, similar stories are told throughout the world, wherever a colonial empire has subdued if not conquered inhabitants of lands rich with material resources.

Too often, economic exploitation and cultural destruction have been legitimated by religious arrogance. This was certainly the case in the Europeanization of North America, where Christianity cloaked the other forces of oppression with a religious superiority that claimed to embody the only Truth.

The Lubicon Cree of Northern Alberta were promised a land settlement in 1939. They are still waiting. As I became involved in the Lubicon struggle for justice, and as I learned about the Dene in the Northwest Territories, I saw first-hand how aboriginal spirituality was demeaned and often destroyed. With their spiritual roots cut away, these peoples found it more difficult to withstand economic marginalization and political deceit.

I was honoured to participate in the General Council of the United Church of Canada in Sudbury in 1986, when moderator and friend Bob Smith presented the Apology to First Nations peoples. This apology represented a significant first step towards healing, though the work of implementation still continues.

But it was the Indian residential school litigation, and the graphic stories that emerged from it, that most opened people's hearts and minds. The personal stories from people who were physically and sexually abused as children in these schools are a continuing disgrace on the record of the Christian churches and of the Canadian government. As moderator, I was involved deeply in the church's attempt to do justice while being the defendant in this legal process. In 1998,

I issued an Apology to Residential School survivors and their families. (See Appendix D, page 213.)

One scene, which symbolizes the old story, stands out in my mind. I attended the opening days of the trial of Blackwater versus the United Church of Canada and the Government of Canada. When I walked into the courtroom in Nanaimo, British Columbia, I saw that the main body of the court was filled with First Nations people, who had travelled great distances to be present. A fence separated these people from all the major players – the judge, the lawyers for the plaintiff and for the defendants (the United Church of Canada and the Government of Canada), the court reporters, and other officials. These latter – the "players" – were all white. The "dominating system" was still in place.

Thankfully, and despite all odds, the governing narratives of First Nations peoples in Canada are making a comeback. We see this reflected in their recovery of language and spiritual traditions, healing circles, renewed forms of governance, and growing confidence. I continue to be humbled as I learn and experience various aspects of the "Native way."

In a similar fashion, aboriginal communities throughout the world are also recovering their stories, which are being celebrated in visual art, dance, song, word, and spiritual practices.

What's particularly exciting to me is that *all* of us are benefiting from the exciting emergence of ancient myth and story coming from aboriginal peoples.

Exile in the Bible

This story of exile and recovery has been repeated throughout history and is basic to the Bible. The Exodus and Exile narratives in the Hebrew Bible are essential to Jewish faith and understanding. Jewish ceremonies and high holidays retell and rehearse these stories to remind the people of who they are. Their strength, resilience, and vision as a people are nurtured and inspired by these and other narratives found in their ancient texts.

In many ways, the Exodus story is the foundational narrative for the Jewish people. Here is my *midrash* (non-literal interpretation) of that story.

The Hebrews were locked in slavery in Egypt under the tyrannical rule of the pharaoh. Whipped by their slave masters, they made bricks in the hot sun. They were beaten down. So, in a far-off land, God summoned Moses, who had been born and raised in Egypt. God told Moses to return to Egypt, to free the Hebrew people.

Moses resisted. God insisted. "What will I say to the pharaoh?" pleaded Moses. God assured Moses that he would be given the necessary words and actions at the required time.

Since God was, after all, God, and since people listened to God in those days, Moses gave in and went back to Egypt.

Moses confronted the pharaoh and named the injustices of the empire. He called on the Hebrew slaves to lay down their tools and walk off the job. I submit that it was the first wildcat strike in human history! Amazingly, they followed Moses in a fantastic exodus from the land of their oppression.

Jewish people tell this story over and over again in their celebrations and worship. The story of God's hand and solidarity in their liberation is crucial to their self-understanding.

Epic stories

Epic stories – whether seen as metaphors, allegories, or exaggerated tales from ancient times – are essential to human self-understanding. Sometimes, people get tangled up in circular debates about whether or not a certain story is "true." This is particularly true when it comes to stories from the Bible. Scholarship from many disciplines helps to shed new light on these foundational stories, but such rigorous examination can also deprive them of their power.

One could argue, for example, that the Bible contains the myths by which Christians and Jews live. These myths may or may not be rooted in historical fact, but in a sense that doesn't matter because their relevance extends far beyond such "provable" events. As myths or guiding narratives, these stories are larger and more profound than the specific events they depict.

J. Edward Chamberlin's book *If This Is Your Land, Where Are Your Stories?* is an original and challenging analysis of the importance of story. It reminds us of how our stories, songs, and poetry (not to mention visual arts and music) give meaning to our lives.

The Christian tradition depends upon the Jesus story. As a Christian, I can and must confess that this story has been co-opted by societies throughout the ages for political, economic, social, and domineering purposes. This co-opting process has occurred within many other faith traditions as well, and contributes to the conflict and misunderstanding we experience today.

National narratives

In the English-speaking world, most people are familiar with the British Empire and the American Dream. Both represent overarching narratives under which many stories give inspiration and form to the United Kingdom and the United States in most aspects of their life.

The British Empire

I grew up in a school system where we were proud of all the pink regions on our maps of the world. Pink was the colour of the British Empire. The British Empire extended its impressive reach to all parts of the globe. As part of the empire, we were proud that Canada had the largest land mass. We were taught that the British Empire brought civilization to the rest of the world. Wherever it went, the "empire project" brought the English language, the rule of English law, extensive trade, Christianity, and the symbols of British culture to indigenous peoples. It created new elites, marginalized if not destroyed host cultures, and extolled all things British. The sun was never to set on the British Empire.

I grew up in a family proud to reinforce the glories of the empire. I remember filling scrapbooks with pictures and stories of the royal family. In Ontario, we celebrated Queen Victoria's birthday with firecrackers, and by opening up the family cottage. We removed shutters from the windows, put canoes into the water, and cleared and swept moth balls from the beds and from the floors. Although I knew little about Queen Victoria herself, I knew she was part of my family's cottage-going and fireworks-watching tradition.

Of course, I was taught little about the ravages of empire. I learned almost nothing about the cultural genocide of First Nations peoples until I moved to Alberta, when I was 41 years old, and found out about the continuing disgrace of the Lubicon Cree in Northern Alberta. In school, I learned about the fur trade, but was told nothing of the mandate of the empire to extract valuable resources from the colonies to enrich the emerging capitalists back "home." The Hudson's Bay Company stands as one example of how commercial power was used as an instrument of political hegemony. One of the first trans-national corporations, it was granted a huge land mass by the Crown, and resembled what we now label a fully vertically integrated company.

The myth of the British Empire included fantastic tales of intrepid explorers surviving the freezing cold of the Arctic and the boiling heat of African jungles. We celebrated the names of the great explorers and their larger-than-life heroics, while we never named, much less acknowledged, the native peoples who rescued them and enabled them to survive.

The narrative of the British Empire encompassed all aspects of life – military, commercial, political, educational, cultural, ecological, and religious. The supposedly superior values and principles it articulated, promoted, and legislated were designed and intended to create a semi-homogenous "culture." Although a few lesser indigenous customs were preserved for show, the main narrative celebrated the conquering of continents and the overcoming of dangerous and exotic obstacles so that the flag of true civilization could be flown in all parts of the world. In the process, enormous wealth was created, and powerful political institutions were installed. Christianity, the "one true religion," declared that God was on the side of empire, as it strove to "win the world for Christ."

The American Dream

The narrative of the American Dream went somewhat differently, although it expressed similar dynamics. This experiment, conducted in the New World, would espouse and enshrine a more egalitarian theme, at least for some. Separation of church and state would frame a social dynamic wherein immigrants from the British Isles, Ireland, and many parts of Europe, would be free from class rigidities, enabling them to pursue their own dreams. Everyone was free to climb the ladder of wealth and independence from oppressive social structures.

Well, not quite everyone. Black slaves and Native Americans need not apply for inclusion in this American Dream. Nevertheless, the United States Constitution was modeled after the new French Republic and the remarkable Iroquois Confederacy. The impulse to democratic institutions, complete with the checks and balances inherent in the Constitution, inspired an energetic people to new heights of wealth and individual opportunity.

Although the attempt to conquer native peoples, the bloody and divisive Civil War, and military adventures overseas revealed a corrosive and vicious reality, the dream of democracy, responsible civic engagement, an independent judiciary, and an energetic and brash entertainment culture survive as part of the American Dream. It can still be a beacon of hope. The scientific imagination, extraordinary universities, eclectic culture, and commercial and financial genius are ongoing expressions of the dream, symbolized by the Statue of Liberty in New York harbour. While the gross distortions, misconduct, and simplistic arrogance of the Bush administration and its industrial henchmen have morphed a compelling dream into a vicious empire, I believe that their delusions of empire will fail, and that the dream will be renewed.

Regardless of how one understands and interprets the British Empire and the American Dream, both represent fundamental narratives by which the British and the Americans lived for two centuries. These stories are embedded in every aspect of their respective cultures.

Since World War II, the British have needed to revise their story – not an easy task. It will be interesting to see if the end of Queen Elizabeth's reign will be a cathartic crossroads in the redefinition of the story of the British Empire.

Similarly, the American Dream will undergo transformation as the seismic effect of the ecological crisis, financial debt, and new international realities sink in. Both stories are due for a drastic rewrite.

The Canadian narrative

Of course, Canada has its own intriguing narrative. Our colonial history tells the story of a struggle between the French and the English, both seeking to extend their commercial and political empires. Both powers viewed the top half of the North American continent as a rich storehouse of natural resources. The supply of fish, timber, furs, minerals, and other resources seemed endless, and ideal for the lucrative European market.

In the process of taming and settling this harsh and vast land, scant attention was paid to the First Peoples, who comprised many nations. If they could help in the grand colonial enterprise, fine. If not, they could be ignored or pushed aside. Treaties were made, but rarely honoured. Residential schools became an instrument of assimilation, and worse, of cultural genocide, as already discussed. While Canada did not suffer the equivalent of the "Indian Wars" that were fought south of the 49th parallel, the conquering of this part of the continent continued in different ways. The price of such white European arrogance is now being paid.

It is only in recent years that Canadians are becoming aware that Canada has more than two founding nations, as has been the rhetoric for centuries. The indigenous peoples of Canada comprise many nations, cultures, languages, and unique histories. While the colonial experience in Canada can be traced to 1497, when John Cabot, sailing under the authority of the English crown, "discovered" Newfoundland – he was followed closely by the French explorer Jacques Cartier, who sailed up the St. Lawrence River in 1534 –First Nations can trace their experience in this land, "Canada," to at least 8,000 BCE and perhaps even further back.

The narratives of indigenous peoples in the many regions of Canada – the Maritimes, central Canada, the prairies, the West Coast, the Arctic, and all the sub-regions – are uniquely distinct from each other. The ways of life, survival challenges, art, trade patterns, and social structures are special to each regional and linguistic group. (The Canadian Canoe Museum in Peterborough, Ontario, displays fascinating maps showing trade patterns of First Nations *before* contact with Europeans. The many amazing rivers and lakes provided an extensive and vast "highway system" for trade and cultural exchanges.)

Of course, understanding the many foundational narratives of First Nations peoples is crucial to understanding their ways of life, key values, and visions of what it is to live in this beautiful, dangerous, and complicated land. A most important "project" in recent years is the recovery of the oral tradition going back thousands of years. The recovery of story and language parallels the recovery of whole peoples and cultures. As this process continues, the Canadian narrative becomes an even more intriguing tapestry of ancient and modern experience.

The governing Canadian narrative, however, involved the back-and-forth struggle between the French and the English for dominance, as well as resistance to the growing American powerhouse to the south. It is a powerful story that has issued in such programs as official bilingualism and biculturalism, and ongoing political tensions and power struggles between Quebec and "the rest of Canada."

More recently, immigration from all parts of the world has exerted pressure to shift the story into a multicultural kaleidoscope of global influences. The official story is becoming more complex and interesting.

The reality of being a northern country with vast expanses of snow and ice, and with seemingly endless forested spaces (as can be found in the Canadian Shield), with untold numbers of rivers, lakes, and mountains – being a country such as this influences our art, literature, music, and sense of adventure in the great outdoors. The image of a solo canoe or kayak on a lonely northern lake, the sound of a loon's haunting call, or a glimpse of a great blue heron rising gracefully through early morning mist – these things are embedded in our collective psyche.

Yet that texture of our story is also changing. Eighty percent of Canadians live in urban areas close to the border with the United States. A significant portion of the population now comes from areas of the world unfamiliar with "the North," or with "cottage country." Camping in the northern parts of the provinces and in the territories is primarily a middle-class white experience.

Of course, in a completely different way, oil and gas reserves have once again turned the attention of the world to the north, which is now seen as a storehouse of resources for the south, primarily for the United States. Of course, little concern is given to the ecological and cultural damage these changes have wrought on fragile systems.

Our Canadian narrative, like the American and British narratives, is undergoing significant change. Yet the stories by which we live still influence who we are and how we will respond to the challenges that lie ahead. The reality is that stories shape who we are and who we wish to be. The big question is this: which of the essential qualities of these stories will we embrace?

New stories, new life

Suffice it to say that if we ignore the overarching and underlying story of our society or culture, we will fail to understand the issues and challenges we face. Without serious reflection on our governing narrative, we will see certain things as inevitable (poverty, for example) and therefore as impossible to change. We will see other things as having no observable cause (for example, some diseases). Only as we begin to see the issues of society (politics, economics, spirituality) within the context of our governing narrative will we be able to develop public policies that can find effective solutions and healthy ways forward.

As I stated at the beginning of this chapter, this is a spiritual issue, for it touches on who we believe we are and how we will relate to each other and to the Earth. In a way, the story of a culture is the spiritual framework in which a culture lives, and moves, and has its being.

I believe the time has come for new, dangerous, and life-giving stories. We need stories that celebrate the amazing biological, racial, and cultural diversity of the Earth, and which, at the same time, illustrate the realities of power, poverty, racism, and all the other ugly things that divide humankind from itself, and from the blessings of the Earth. New stories lead to new understandings, which lead to new agendas, which lead to life abundant. We need new stories to put us in touch with the mystery of life, with its beauty, possibility, danger, and opportunity; with its love, compassion, and tenderness. But first, let's look at the old story.

Discussion Questions

1. Do you believe societies live out a story or a narrative that can be described and understood?

2. If so, what influence or import do you think these stories have on economics, politics, faith, relationships, and the way we live?

3. Do you agree with the way I characterized the stories of First Nations and colonial powers, biblical people, the British Empire, the United States, and Canada?

4. If not, how would you describe the narrative of these societies?

5. In what ways do you find the idea of "story" helpful in addressing the crossroads we face?

3. The Old Story

Every society lives out its prevailing myth, story, or narrative. This story creates the parameters within which all aspects of life are lived, from education to commerce to politics. Often, religion nurtures the governing narrative, or at least allows it to maintain its hold on both the conscious and the unconscious, the individual and the collective mind.

Our society is in the grip of an increasingly destructive narrative, what I call the Old Story. Some scholars say that this story is at least 5000 years old. Others say that it is newer than that.

When I give workshops on this theme, I ask participants to name the characteristics of the Old Story. It is interesting what they come up with. Here is a list of words and phrases they use to describe their experience of the Old Story.

They say that it is characterized by

» unbalanced power

» entitlement

» hubris

» corruption

» fear

» greed

» competitiveness

» short-sighted
    solutions

» and conquest;

that it values such things as

» control

» the easy life

» convenience

» fresh fruit all year

» "free trade"

» and celebrity;

that it believes

» war brings peace

» it is beyond or above
    the law

» growth is a virtue

» bigger is better

and that it leads to

» over-packaging
and "supersizing"
» blaming the victim

» a throw-away culture
» global warming
» mindless suburbia.

These people *know* the toxic qualities that lead to the breakdown of communities and to the destruction of the Earth – a significant point in and of itself, and one I'll return to at the end of the chapter. For now, however, I want to look at the Old Story in more detail.

The basic thrust of the Old Story is that human beings stand "above" nature, as the masters of creation. Nevertheless, we exist in a perpetual state of competition and struggle for power. Both of these aspects of the Old Story are founded on the patriarchal myth of male superiority and control. *Its* characteristics are violence, domination, arrogance, and competition.

Put all this together, and the Old Story manifests itself as ecological destruction; disrespect; an insatiable appetite for power; war and the obscene military expenditures that go with it; rampant and unprecedented consumerism; a growing gap between rich and poor; and intrigue and mistrust of time-honoured institutions, such as governments, corporations, unions, religions, and universities. In the last 25 years in particular, runaway greed, attacks upon the vulnerable, and the poisoning of the Earth have all contributed to the growth of a sense of entitlement and, at the same time, of fear.

Ecological destruction

Bill Rees, who teaches at the University of British Columbia, talks about our ecological footprint. He says,

> Every culture has its myths, and right now, our myth is so powerful that it prevents us from facing the truth. For us to maintain our way of living, we must tell lies to each other and especially to ourselves. The lies are necessary because without them, many deplorable acts would become impossibilities. In other words, the truth would stop us from doing stupid things.[1]

The consequences of these lies are many. For example, in the last 200 years, the United States has lost 50 percent of its wetlands, 90 percent of its old growth forests, and 99 percent of its tall grass prairies.

A citizen of a so-called advanced industrial nation consumes in six months the energy that has to last a citizen in a developing country their entire life. In developing countries, land is often expropriated for huge dams, or to grow monoculture crops (almost always at the demand of international organizations, such as the World Bank), or to raise cattle for fast food chains. As a result, peasant farmers flee the land and flood into the cities, where they live in squalor, their young women expropriated for the sex trade. North American appetites may be fed, and its stock markets may go up, but the living conditions of millions go down.

In North America, urban sprawl is not only unsustainable, it uses up resources, creates alienation, and is aesthetically nauseating. Monster homes built on prime farm land, away from public transit and other essential services, boast three-car garages, every possible "amenity," and country living (which of course is nonsense). I grew up in the 1950s, in a family of four, in a nice, middle-class (some would say wealthy) neighbourhood in north Toronto. Our house had three good-sized bedrooms, a fireplace, and enough space to suit our needs. Our yard had beautiful oak and maple trees. We lived close to reliable public transit. I could walk to school.

The average home size has doubled since then, and the car has become almost a necessity, unless one lives downtown.

Of course, not all was well, even back in the 1950s. In Toronto, urban sprawl was in its early heyday. As the city grew, I watched it chew up valuable farm land and stretch itself beyond the reach of affordable public services. Now I live in Calgary, where I'm watching the same phenomenon happen all over again. We have learned very little, it appears. Developers say, "People want their own piece of land." So we pave our way to the Rockies and to Montana, believing it is our "right."

I remember preaching a sermon in Toronto about how we are paving over the world. At that time, the marvellously fertile land of the Niagara Peninsula was under severe threat from "development." The orchards and vineyards of the Niagara area are renowned for their succulent and tasty fruit. Yet the bulldozers and paving machines always lurked on the horizon, ready to attack. I imaged archeologists in the year 3000 exploring the area. They would roll up the pavement, peer down at the rich soil, and exclaim, "No wonder these people starved to death!"

Entitlement and consumer society

Much if not most of the damage we are doing to the environment is directly related to our sense of entitlement and to the consumer culture we have created to support and feed it.

Of course, the advertising industry fuels our consumerist ways. How many times do advertisers tell us, "You deserve..." Too often I hear people say, "If I can afford it (or if I can max out my credit cards), I am entitled to it." So we build monster homes, buy fast cars, take exotic trips, and purchase every available electronic gadget, believing we are entitled to spend and do what we want.

Unfortunately for the planet, and therefore unfortunately for us, while all those products we "deserve" may pamper us, in their production and use they are also destroying the planet. To satisfy our desires, huge machines clear-cut forests, drag oceans, and mine the Earth. The sheer scale of production today is far beyond what the Earth can withstand. Fishing boats are one thing. Fleets of factory trawlers are something else again.

Each of us has our own list of things that make us shake our heads. The "throw away" culture, which consumerism inspires, is one of my pet peeves. It's everywhere, from the 30 million plastic water bottles we throw away each day, to the over-packaging I encounter every time I buy something, and which contributes to the overflow of our disappearing landfill sites. The most annoying is the hard plastic covering used on almost everything from combs to screw drivers. For me, over-packaging is the most poignant and daily symbol of a wasteful culture.

Our sense of entitlement extends to the foods we eat. When I was a child growing up in Toronto, my parents did their weekly shopping at the St. Lawrence Market. They bought from local farmers, whom they came to know. Vegetables were placed in brown paper bags, which we used later for school lunches. With the exception of citrus fruits not grown in Canada, we ate fresh fruit only when it was in season. This practise made waiting for strawberries and field tomatoes almost a spiritual discipline, and the fruit, when it arrived, that much more special.

Today, the Old Story tells us that we are entitled to eat any kind of food we want, anywhere, at any time of the year.

With that mandate, we transport food thousands of kilometres, from all over the world, all year round, consuming untold quantities of fuel and increasing global warming.

The Old Story tells us that we are entitled to consume all we want, in whatever manner suits us. Our economic system seems to depend upon the endless extension and expansion of whatever our greedy minds can dream up and our advancing technology can deliver. I exaggerate only a little when I say that our culture of entitlement feeds our greed rather than meets our needs.

Disconnection from the Earth

According to Ronald Wright in *A Short History of Progress*, the downfall of many civilizations over the past 5000 years has been the human addiction to using available technology on increasingly larger scales. So, as I pointed out above, if we can clear-cut a forest, we will. If we can use huge trawlers to catch cod, we will. But our mega-fishing is de-populating the world's oceans. Populations of predatory fish – tuna, bullfish, swordfish, and cod fish to name a few – have declined by 90 percent since the beginning of industrial fishing in the 1960s. Industrial fishing practices have collapsed or put in serious decline 13 of the 17 major ocean fisheries.

A famous Cree saying speaks volumes: "Only when the last tree has died and the last river has been poisoned and the last fish has been caught will we realize that we cannot eat money."

William Sloane Coffin, that great Christian prophet of contemporary America, says that, "We are beginning to resemble extinct dinosaurs who suffered from far too much armour and too little brain." I would add that we also suffer from too little spiritual grounding in the Earth, and in all that nurtures life.

As a species, we have become separated from our sacred relationship with the Earth; we have become alien to the Earth. We see ourselves as masters over creation, or as "stewards" of creation. Although the words "steward" and "stewardship" have a long history, and have helped us care for and share resources in the past, they can be problematic when used in regard to our relationship with the Earth. They imply that humankind is in charge of ensuring the health and well-being of the planet. The concept of stewardship makes *us* and *our* values the focus of everything we do. Granted, we often act with the best of intentions. Yet I believe we need to emphasize in every way possible that *the Earth is not ours.* Rather, *we belong to the Earth*; we are creatures *of* the Earth, just like all other living things. We are merely one strand in the web of being that is the Earth. In fact, we are far more dependent upon the Earth than the Earth is dependent upon us. Yet we poison its rivers, foul its air, and destroy its habitats, all of which reduce biological diversity. No wonder we feel alone, isolated, set adrift.

Where I live, in Calgary, the dominant white society has a great love of nature. In fact, the natural beauty that surrounds the city is one of its great attractions. People love the "outdoors," the mountains and the rivers. They excel in skiing, hiking, climbing, and paddling. Yet the tremendous monetary wealth "enjoyed" here, which allows all this outdoor recreation, depends upon extractive industries, which carve up, plunder, poison, and denude the Earth. More often than not, they also destroy indigenous cultures, along with their stories of living with respect in creation.

Why this deep disconnect between our love of nature, the wonder of the Earth, and our addiction to economic systems bent on destruction? I wish I knew. Maybe we're like the smoker who knows his addiction is bad for his health, and costly, but can't or won't stop smoking. Or maybe it's because of our sense of entitlement. Perhaps we feel the Earth and its resources exist for *our* exclusive, unlimited use? Or maybe it's because of our faith in technology, our belief that technology will find solutions to our near-sighted stupidity? Or because of our addiction to an economic system predicated on growth?

Why this deep disconnect?

I *do* know that most religions and spiritual traditions teach that the Earth is sacred. In the biblical creation story in Genesis, the Divine Energy of Creation proclaims that the Earth and all its creatures are good. The Bible begins with the river of life flowing out into the world from the Garden of Eden, and ends with it flowing into the City of God, where it waters the Tree of Life.

For Black Elk and indigenous people, the Earth is sacred Mother, holding in her embrace all trees, grasses, insects, animals, rivers, mountains, and birds.

Genuine peace and real prosperity come in the human soul when we recognize and celebrate our oneness, our interdependence with all the Creator's creatures. The Earth is indeed full of wonder, mystery, and life, in all its glorious manifestations. The Earth is truly awesome. The Earth is sacred. Yet we live in a secular, hyper-consumerist, anti-intellectual, market-driven, "security"-obsessed, plundering, alienating, and self-destructive society.

The rich get richer while the poor get poorer

Stephen Lewis begins his book *Race Against Time* with the words, "I have spent the last four years watching people die. Nothing in my adult life prepared me for the carnage of HIV/AIDS." He concludes the book with a question: "Can someone please explain to me our contemporary balance of values?"[2]

I read Lewis' book the day after our church housed "Inn from the Cold," a ministry offered by 60 congregations in Calgary that provide shelter for homeless people on a rotating basis. Of the 15 homeless people who slept on cots in our gym that Friday night, six were children. Calgary is one of the wealthiest places on Earth. This homelessness is an obscenity. It reminded me of the ongoing disgrace of our treatment of the Lubicon Cree in Northern Alberta.

The Lubicon were promised a reserve in 1939. By an oversight of the government of Canada, they had been left out of the previous Treaty (Treaty 8), which promised land and resources. Today, the Lubicon continue to negotiate with both federal and provincial governments.

Ever since oil and gas were discovered on their land, the area has been ripped apart. As a result, the Lubicon's traditional economy, culture, and spiritual practices have all but been destroyed. Meanwhile, more than $13 billion worth of oil and gas has been taken from their land. The Lubicon have received nothing. Not surprisingly, tuberculosis, alcohol and drug abuse, suicide, and unemployment have all soared among the Lubicon.

When people learn about the ongoing Lubicon tragedy, they are appalled. Yet no public outcry and no strategy so far has moved governments sufficiently for justice to be done. Since 1983, I have participated in commissions of inquiry, boycotts, blockades, workshops, demonstrations, briefings, presentations to government, and speech-making. Still the cultural genocide identified by the World Council of Churches in 1983 continues. This conscious neglect and exploitation of a First Nations people is a national disgrace.

The obscenity of children dying by the thousands each day from preventable diseases; of people unable to afford privatized water or basic housing; of indigenous people seeing their land, culture, language, and economies destroyed in the name of globalization; these obscenities are matched at the other end by the obscenity of the super rich.

One day, two bankers strode into a famous London establishment. They asked the bartender to make them the most expensive cocktail he could concoct. So he blended a Richard Hennessy cognac (at $5,150 per bottle), Dom Perignon champagne, lemongrass, lychees and yohiche bark (a West African import with aphrodisiac power). He called it the Magic Noir and charged $500 per glass. The final bill for a table of 8, according to the article in *The Guardian Weekly*[3] which reported it, was $25,000.

Another example caught my attention when I was leafing through a magazine on an airplane. It was an advertisement showing a man lying on the road with his head smashed in, his glasses broken, and a boot print on the side of his head. The caption read, "Our apologies to the meek and the world they shall not inherit – in the market you either kick or get kicked." Ironically, this full-page advertisement was placed

BILL PHIPPS | **85** | *The Old Story*

by a software company. It ranks as the most grotesque image and text I have ever seen in a magazine. Not only was it violent, it played on one of the most profound and challenging statements made by Jesus in his so-called Sermon on the Mount, in that section called "The Beatitudes." I might have dismissed this revolting ad as an aberration had it not appeared in one of the most highly respected and widely read business magazines in the world. Another ad in the same magazine screamed, "Don't just compete. Conquer!" I was looking at the Old Story in very stark terms.

The military-industrial complex

We see this desire to conquer and to crush most clearly in the pathological actions of the military-industrial complex and its war-mongering ways. I once labelled the Bush administration as "weak men on steroids." Showing no imagination in the world of diplomacy and international relations, it is (was) the gross epitome of a violent, arrogant, macho story being told in millions of ways, from the local sports bar to the killing fields of Iraq, Sudan, and Afghanistan. It is a story that includes child soldiers, and raped girls and women caught in endless civil wars.

Clearly, the military-industrial complex, that deadly poisonous mixture President Eisenhower (a Republican) warned about, has the world in its grip. Ike once said,

> Every gun that is made, every warship launched, every rocket fired signifies in the final sense, a theft from those who hunger and are not fed, those who are cold and are not clothed. This world in arms is not spending money alone. It is spending the sweat of its laborers, the genius of its scientists, the hopes of its children. This is not a way of life at all in any true sense. Under the clouds of war, it is humanity hanging on a cross of iron.

I name the United States because of its incredible and unprecedented power. Yet the U.S. is only the most obvious example of a story most of us are living. Everyone knows that for the price of one aircraft carrier, a few fighter jets, one ill-conceived war in Iraq, everyone in Africa could have clean water, drugs to combat AIDS, free education, and health care. The war in Iraq, by the way, costs approximately $2,500 per second, or $250 million per day. Of course, we also know that no government will ever run up a huge deficit to accomplish such laudable goals. But shouldn't we at least be asking questions when such staggering expenditures are made to fight a "war on terror," or on any other convenient enemy? How much more in the grip of an old, soul- and Earth-destroying story could we be?

The culture of fear

War-mongering and fear-mongering go hand-in-hand, and governments and media seem to collaborate in both. It has gotten to the point that, today, we fear just about everything. A June 26, 2006, headline in the *Calgary Sun* screamed in big bold letters, "SCARED TO THE CORE... Nearly half of Calgarians afraid of downtown LRT [Light Rapid Transit] platforms."

Despite the fact that the rate of violent crime in North America has remained basically unchanged in 20 years, or has been reduced dramatically in some places – in New York City, for example – the media's mindless reporting of violent incidents both at home and abroad convinces people that life is dangerous. And so we spend billions of dollars building gated communities, enhancing border security, and engaging in domestic spying.

People who are afraid are more easily controlled and manipulated. Unfortunately, it's not just governments who know this. Religions know it too. Too much of Old-Story Christianity is fear-based. Fear of going to hell has given the religious establishment all kinds of levers with which to manipulate people. Some expressions of faith rely on fear and guilt to extract money, as well as promises and specified behaviours, from people. It is difficult to believe in a God of unconditional love, grace, goodness, and generosity, when his or her agents dwell on guilt, angry judgment, and the "badness" of people.

Fear pervades Western society. Fear of terrorist attacks. Fear of the inner city. Fear of not having enough. Fear of disaster. Fear of life itself. As a result, beauty is trumped by ugliness. Generosity dissolves into greed. Compassion recedes into isolation. Health deteriorates into illness. Trust is inverted to suspicion. And everywhere, the common good is ignored. Fear becomes a cloak under which we hide from life and its basic abundance, wonder, and opportunity.

Cause for hope

At the beginning of this chapter, I said that when I ask workshop participants to name the characteristics of the Old Story, they are well able to do it. It is clear that we *know* the self-destructive, dead-end destination of the Old Story. We *know* we are living a death-dealing story. Perhaps most importantly, we know that the Old Story has almost run its course.

For me, this represents a profound cause for hope, because *once we are conscious of the Old Story, we can consciously choose a different story.* What's more, just as we know the characteristics of the Old Story, I believe we know the characteristics of a New Story, whose narrative can redeem our hearts, and bring healing and justice to the world.

Discussion Questions

1. Do you agree with my characterization of the Old Story?

2. How would you describe the narrative we are living? Which of these characteristics seem particularly "old" to you?

3. Is the Old Story entirely negative, or are parts of it positive and worth saving? Name any parts you think are positive.

4. How and where do you experience "fear" in your life?

1 Bill Rees, *Adbusters*, September-October 2004.
2 Stephen Lewis, *Race Against Time* (Toronto: House of Anansi Press, 2005), 1, 189.
3 *The Guardian Weekly* (December 2–8, 2005), R5.

4. The New Story

Just as people who take my workshops are able to name the key aspects of the Old Story, they are also able to name the features of the New Story. Here are some of the words and phrases they use to describe their experience of the New Story.

They say that it is

» relationship-centred

» non-violent

» child-honouring

» mindful

» and sustainable;

that it is characterized by

>> wonder

>> respect

>> cooperation

>> longing

>> laughter

>> humility

>> empowerment

>> interdependence

>> interconnection

>> abundance

>> and gratitude;

that it values such things as

>> dialogue

>> listening

>> community

>> honouring each other

>> consensus

>> harmony

>> creation and God

>> dignity

>> recycling

>> minimalism

>> and "fair" trade;

and that it believes

>> slow is good, and

>> small is beautiful.

Just as we *know* the destructive essence of the Old Story, we *know* the life-giving characteristics of the New Story. Let's look at some of these characteristics in more detail.

The new narrative is rooted in spiritual values found in most faith traditions. David Hallman reflects on some of these values in his book *Spiritual Values for Earth Community*. Specifically, he names gratitude, humility, sufficiency, justice, peace, love, faith, and hope. In other words, the New Story recognizes the inviolable interconnection between economics, politics, community, and spirituality. It understands that issues of violence, poverty, racism, heterosexism, and ecological disintegration are deeply related; and that the old method of isolating issues from each other in a divide-and-conquer way is no longer possible if we are serious about wanting transformation. In concrete terms, this often leads to a commitment to cooperation, mutuality, respect, local control, and international law and conventions.

Wonder

Although it may be less obvious than some of the characteristics named above, I believe that *wonder* is a key quality that lies within the creative imagination of the New Story. Wonder takes us out of ourselves, allowing us to celebrate and to stand in genuine awe before a world of mystery. It reminds us that we are not in control of everything and are called to deep appreciation of the Earth's complexity and secrets. Wonder reflects humility rather than hubris. It causes us to marvel at the astonishing beauty of the Earth and leads us to infinite exploration.

Wonder inspires us to recognize that we are part of the natural order. We are creatures of the Earth, not masters over it. This recognition results in a whole new understanding of our relationships with one another, with other creatures, and with the Earth itself.

Gratitude

Wonder also leads naturally to gratitude. When we live with gratitude, we see life as a gift to be lived as fully as possible. When we are thankful for the Earth's mysterious, enriching, and precious gifts, we are more likely to live lives of generosity. Our sense of entitlement gives way to sharing and conversation.

All of us know people who are *grateful* for everything they have and who are *generous* with everything they have. We also know people who complain about what they *don't* have and are miserly as a result. If we understand ourselves to be in a partnership, living in mutual interdependence with all other life forms, then our behaviours will automatically change to reflect this new mindset.

Abundance

A sense of abundance is part of this new mindset. In fact, abundance, gratitude, and wonder are all part of the dance leading to true fullness of life.

The saying that the "Earth provides enough for everyone's need, but not for everyone's greed" is true. The Earth provides abundantly. Within its delicate environmental envelope, the Earth breathes life into billions of life forms, regenerates itself, and provides sustenance for all its creatures.

Yet our economic systems, cheered on by advertising, convince us that we never have enough, and that we need to get for ourselves while the getting is good. With a mentality of scarcity, we tend to hoard, compete, and collect for fear that nothing will be left.

On the other hand, a mentality of abundance leads to greater sharing and respect for the "commons." For example, it can lead us to view taxes as the way we share our common wealth, rather than as a confiscation of what is "mine." A friend once described the economy as the way in which we love each other collectively. Currently, we love each other very badly, our economic structures being what they are. But it doesn't have to be that way. We can choose to share our wealth. The attitude that will allow this to happen grows out of gratitude for the Earth's abundance, and our joy in sharing its goodness.

Partnership

These characteristics of the New Story are reflected in Riane Eisler's notion of partnership in all areas of our lives.

In her wonderful guidebook on living a new narrative, *The Power of Partnership*, Eisler contrasts domination living with partnership living. For example, in the category of social structure, the domination model is characterized by an "authoritarian structure of rigid rankings and hierarchies of domination," whereas the partnership model features an "egalitarian structure of linking..." In the category of belief systems, in the domination model "relations of control/domination [are] presented as normal, desirable, and moral," whereas in the partnership model, "relations of partnership/respect [are] presented as normal, desirable, and moral." The domination model encourages fear, violence, and male domination. The partnership model promotes mutual trust, acceptance, non-violence, and equal valuing of men and women.

The contrasting models of domination or partnership can be applied to all aspects of human living – politics, economics, family relationships, education, ethics, work, and religion. The New Story embodies the life-affirming and freedom-giving characteristic of the partnership model Eisler describes.

Moments of grace

In Chapter 1, I referred to Thomas Berry's book *The Great Work*. Berry begins a chapter called "Moments of Grace" this way: "As we enter the twenty-first century, we are experiencing a moment of grace. Such moments are privileged moments. The great transformation of the universe occurs at such times."

I do believe that this period of history is full of grace, possibility, and opportunity. We can choose to be overcome by dread, fear, or denial. In fact, many people live out this option every day. But as spiritual beings, as people with an ancient story with contemporary resonance, as people living with other people of faith or with people who share our dreams and who support us in this rapid river run, we can instead choose a new story of hope.

Transformation – my story

Of course, shifting mental, spiritual, political, and economic gears (to only name a few) is not easy. Often, it requires some direct personal experience of a different culture or way of being in the world. At least, that's how it happened for me.

In the summer of 1964, after my second year at Osgoode Hall Law School in Toronto, I got a job as the assistant director of a children's program at Lafayette Avenue Presbyterian Church in Brooklyn, New York. Lafayette is an old, historic church noted for many things, including being the place where the Emancipation Proclamation was drafted after the American Civil War.

In the 1960s, the neighbourhood was in a state of racial and economic transition. It straddled the border between Brooklyn Heights and Bedford Stuyvesant, one of the poorest Black communities in the United States.

George Litch Knight was one of the ministers. He was a flamboyant literary man and lover of the arts. (He introduced me to off-Broadway theatre, jazz clubs, and many other delights of New York City. It is still my favourite city in the world.)

He was also one of the strangest characters I have ever met, full of contradictions, sensitivities, and bombast. Certainly he was passionate about economic justice and racial equality. He was very bright and, I think, found it difficult to tolerate what he saw as incompetence. I remember staff meetings in the Cuyler Library, where the Emancipation Proclamation was drafted. George could be solicitously encouraging or he could blow up. The reason, of course, was that he cared deeply about people, the community, and the mission of the church. He died in 1997. The plaque in the sanctuary reads

GEORGE LITCH KNIGHT 1925–1997
SIXTH PASTOR OF LAFAYETTE AVENUE PRESBYTERIAN CHURCH,
1957 – 1989
HYMNOLOGIST, HISTORIAN, HUMANITARIAN.
HE MINISTERED TO THE "LAST, THE LOST AND THE LEAST IN HIS
BELOVED BROOKLYN
"…A FRIEND OF… SINNERS…" LUKE 7:34

The church hired university students like myself from across the United States and from Canada. There were two of us from Canada that year. Our job was to run programs for children.

That summer changed my life on so many levels. Here I was, a middle-class white kid (I was 22 years old), plopped into a racially changing neighbourhood dealing with extreme poverty. I had a lot to learn. It was the first summer of the urban riots in the U.S., and the war in Vietnam was starting. I remember National Guard troops at every intersection after parts of Harlem and Bedford-Stuyvesant went up in smoke.

I also remember being one of three white people among 15,000 black people trying to hear Elijah Muhammad at an arena in Harlem. Co-founder of the Black Muslims (also known as the Nation of Islam), Elijah Muhammad was an emerging leader in the African-American community throughout the United States. Appealing to the sense that previous leaders and philosophies had failed to deliver equality and freedom, he inspired people with words and actions rooted in Islam.

Some of us on the summer staff heard that Muhammad

was speaking on Sunday afternoon June 28. What an opportunity to listen, to learn, and to increase our understanding of this growing Black Muslim movement! My journal entry for that day reads,

> We were the only whites there – all the rest were Negro (Remember, this is 1964!). We tried many times to get admitted to the arena, but were gently turned away. It made us know what it is like. The only other white person we saw was another Canadian, from Nova Scotia. It was a funny feeling being among all those Negroes – 15,000 – and being rejected. They were very polite, but cold and impregnable.

Those experiences, plus getting to know an African-American social worker from Mississippi who was on our staff, began a long and steep learning curve for me in the area of race relations.

Many other experiences from that time remain fresh in my mind. One, however, stands out as a moment of truth. I thought later that it was similar to Thomas Merton's experience in Lexington, Kentucky. It was a moment when time stood still, when all of life was integrated.

It happened one morning in August. I emerged from the subway at Lafayette Avenue and South Oxford Street into the hot and steamy atmosphere of Brooklyn. I had done this for more than three months. I was one block from the church.

Lined with old "brownstone" row houses and graced by leafy trees, which provided some shade from the oven heat, South Oxford Street is typical of many Brooklyn streets in residential neighbourhoods. Part of our summer program featured games on the street. I came to love the feel of the street – its age, the people sitting on the steps of the brownstones enjoying quiet conversation, the children playing games, the man drinking from a brown paper bag. But this day it was different.

As I walked up the steps out of the subway, everything seemed to stop – time, movement, traffic, sound. For a few moments, everything and everyone became an integrated part of the whole. The whole world was in harmony, at peace. It was like a movie that had stopped while everyone was embracing. I understood that I, Bill Phipps, was not separate. Even in the hustle of that amazing city, I felt myself to be an integral part of this great bundle of life on our fragile, Earthly home.

The experience was mysterious, deeply profound, and unforgettably real. As I said, that summer transformed me on many levels.

Symbols of hope

Transformation is never easy and it's seldom painless. Which is one reason why the Old Story will not give up easily. As the New Story emerges, the old one rears its head to protest and to protect itself at all costs. Often, we hear voices proclaim that the New Story is merely "quaint," or that it is "naïve," or "typically idealistic." Yet there are many people who are showing through their writings that the New Story is anything but naïve or unrealistic. These people challenge us to live the New Story. Among these prophets are Thomas Berry, Sallie McFaque, Thomas Hartmann, David Korten, David Hallman, Riane Eisler, Vandava Shiva, and Bruce Sanguin.

From another perspective, Thich Nhat Hanh, the Vietnamese Buddhist monk, writes in his book *Peace Is Every Step* that, "We need to protect the ecology of the mind." Creating a culture of peace, an integral part of the New Story, will help rid our minds and hearts of the pollution induced by a culture of aggression and violence.

Other people are living out the New Story in very concrete ways.

Twelve years ago, a 12-year-old boy named Craig Kielburger, from Thornhill, Ontario, started a global campaign to rescue children from slave labour. In 2006 alone, Free the Children, the organization he founded and still runs with his brother Marc, raised $6.5 million. Ninety-three percent of this money goes directly into their projects. One of their goals is educating children. Since starting Free the Children, they have built 425 primary schools for 35,000 pupils in 23 countries. They have also provided well water for 100,000 children. These are the results of only two of their health, education, and justice programs.

Craig and Marc's 2006 book *Me to We* is "a guide to creating 'a revolution in giving and community-building,' and to achieving 'happiness by helping others.'" This is not just a question of charity for them. They want to change people's ideas about what it means to live socially responsible lives. In short, they want to create a genuine shift from "me" to "we."[1] Craig received the 2006 World Children's Prize, also called the "Children's Nobel Prize." Recipients of the prize are nominated by the children of the world, and the cheque is presented by Queen Silvia of Sweden.

Clearly, the Keilburger brothers are part of the movement to write a new narrative.

So is Leah Kazinsky. Twenty years old now, Kazinky lives in Victoria, British Columbia. When she was 18, she learned firsthand about the relationship between mother's milk in the Arctic and the polluting, poisoning practices of the south. Specifically, startling studies had revealed that breast milk found in remote regions of the Arctic contained PCBs and other chemicals used in manufacturing processes in the south. Cancers were developing and mothers were encouraged not to breastfeed their babies. These studies were among the first to illustrate how far pollutants can travel, effecting people nowhere near the poisoning industry.

Kazinsky's new awareness stimulated her to become involved in ecological issues. In an article in the *Globe and Mail* she is quoted as saying, "There is no specific enemy here; we are interconnected as a species and a planet, and are all in this boat together. Today I don't simply want change. I *am* the change I want to see in the world."[2]

Deborah Kershner, violinist, writer, and friend, put both the challenge and her willingness to accept it this way, in a

Walrus magazine article: "I can take the risk of navigating the geography of beauty."

Hope for the future

The New Story is being written and lived by individuals and in communities and movements all over the world. To some extent, it still exists beneath the power and the "radar" of Old Story domination. Yet that is changing. The more we expose the moral bankruptcy of the Old Story, particularly as it pertains to the environment, while at the same time articulating and living the New Story in whatever ways we are able, the more we will become part of a great turning.

The poet and artist Judy Chicago expresses the dream:

And then all that has divided us will merge.

And then compassion will be wedded to power.

And then softness will come to a world that is often harsh and unkind.

And then both women and men will be gentle.

And then both men and women will be strong.

And then no other person will be subject to another's will.

And then all will be rich and varied.

And then all will share equally in the Earth's abundance.

And then all will care for the sick and the weak
   and the old.

And then all will nourish the young.

And then all will cherish life's creatures.

And then all will live in harmony with each other
   and the Earth.

And then everywhere will be called Eden once again.[3]

Discussion Questions

1. Do you agree that we need a New Story by and in which to live? Why?

2. Do you believe that a New Story can lead us into new, just, and Earth-friendly practices and public policy?

3. If so, what characteristics of the New Story do you think are most important, in terms of helping this transformation to come about?

4. What are some inspiring examples from your own life, experience, or observations that you can share?

---

1 "The Keilburger Crusade," *thestar.com*, October 26, 2006.

2 *The Globe and Mail*, October 4, 2005.

3 Judy Chicago, *The Dinner Party: A Symbol of Our Heritage* (New York: Anchor Books, 1979).

5. The New Story as Integrating Narrative

In the previous chapter, I said that the New Story recognizes the inviolable interconnection between economics, politics, community, and spirituality, and I offered examples of people who are writing about and living out this New-Story dynamic. Because this is such a key aspect of the New Story, I would like to explore further the New Story as integrating narrative in this chapter.

Of course, the reason I need to spend so much time on this is because the Old Story, the story most of us have grown up with and know best, communicates a very different message. Those who live according to the Old Story – and that means most of us in at least some areas of our lives – tend to isolate issues in a divide-and-conquer sort of way.

The roots of this tendency are many and deep, and include the mechanistic worldview and scientific rationalism that have defined the last 300 years. According to this worldview, the way to address a problem is to break it down into smaller and smaller bits, and then to "fix" the one "bit" you think is defective.

We see aspects of this tendency everywhere, but nowhere more clearly than in education and medicine. In both education and medicine, specialization has become the name of the game. "General Arts" education in university, or even education for its own sake, is a thing of the past. Why? As author and urban guru Jane Jacobs points out, higher education has turned into "credentialing." Education needs to be specialized in order for the "customer" to get a job. (Yes, I actually heard a university board member call students "customers." How revolting!)

Specialization is equally pronounced in medicine. As a minister giving pastoral care, I often heard patients complain that one specialist didn't know what the other specialist was doing or prescribing. Each doctor, from his or her own specialty, embarked upon a course of treatment with little regard for other medical problems, or for the patient *as a whole.*

Given the scientific and mechanistic worldview we've inherited, and given our culture's demand for specialization, it's no wonder our first inclination is to "isolate" problems and difficult issues. Yet I believe that this approach is no longer viable. We must learn to actually *live* what we say when we declare that all things are interrelated, that all things exist as interdependent parts of the vast web of life. If we are to survive, we must learn to see the planetary system, including humankind and all of our activities, *as a whole.*

Our Earthly home is made up of billions of intersecting beings, each dependent upon and connected to the others. This means, for example, that while the tar sands developments in Alberta may extract huge amounts of oil and create thousands of jobs, they also affect First Nations culture (in negative ways), produce greenhouse gases and pollution and upset the ecological balance in general, which in turn causes illness, which increases the demand on medical services, which... You get the idea.

Too often in scenarios such as this, the people who are working for social justice and for jobs have little to do with the "environmentalists" who are trying to protect species and prevent habitat loss. Traditionally, both groups have mistrusted each other and have actually worked against each other. Social and economic justice has rarely been on the environmental agenda, and the converse is true also.

Racism, economics, and ecology

Author James Cone touches on the Old Story when he writes that this separation is unfortunate because the common enemy is human domination of nature and of each other.[1] Cone goes on to assert that racism is profoundly interrelated with other evils, including the degradation of the Earth. As an example, he notes that the majority of toxic waste produced in the United States is dumped in black neighbourhoods, or in developing countries that need the "trade."

In other words, racism and poverty are not just social justice issues, they are ecological issues. In fact, ecology touches all aspects of human living.

Exchanging the gifts of the Earth

The early 20th-century Lebanese mystic Kahlil Gibran put the notion of the intimate relationship between ecology and economics in an interesting way. The following quotation is from his book *The Prophet*:

> To you the Earth yields her fruit, and you shall not want if you know how to fill your hands.
>
> It is in exchanging the gifts of the Earth that you shall find abundance and be satisfied.
>
> Yet unless the exchange be in love and kindly justice, it will but lead some to greed and others to hunger.[2]

This quotation illustrates well the idea that the Earth is abundant and generous. It can provide more than enough to meet every person's physical, mental, artistic, vocational, and spiritual *needs* – though, significantly, not enough for everyone's *greed*. Rather than a truncated notion of scarcity, our economy should be based upon the freeing notion of abundance leading to equality and dignity. It should be built on generosity and community rather than on greed and self-centredness.

Gibran also assumes the positive existence of trade, the exchange of the Earth's bounty. No doubt he would question the lopsided trade arrangements of current globalization, but he assumes that humans *do* need to exchange the fruits of the Earth. It is *equal exchange* that will bring satisfaction.

But there is a further ethical kicker or qualifier. The exchange must be done in "love and kindly justice." Just like the economy of our family households, at the heart of the global economy there has to be love. In other words, the justice required involves not only strict adherence to the rules. A just exchange of the Earth's resources requires the human qualities of compassion, mercy, and respect. Otherwise, Gibran says, we reap greed for the few and hunger for the many – an accurate description of the current state of the world. If we are to live in harmony with the natural environment, our political and economic systems and priorities will need to reflect Gibran's wisdom and insight.

The economy/ecology connection

The words "ecology" and "economy" come from the same root – specifically, the Greek word for "household." There is an intimate relationship between a society's economy and its ecology. Indeed, one cannot separate, as we conveniently try to do, ecological integrity, economic viability, political policy, true spirituality, and social ethics. Just as biodiversity is essential in nature and a sign of a healthy natural environment, the ability to recognize diverse interests and the intimate connections among our various fields of activity is essential in human communities and a sign of a healthy human social environment.

The Rwandan genocide of 1994 stands as perhaps the most heart-rending and horrific example of the interplay of racism, war, poverty, history, and the presence or absence of "valuable" resources. In the introduction to his book *Shake Hands with the Devil*, Romeo Dallaire declares that the story of Rwanda is one of

> betrayal, failure, naiveté, indifference, hatred, genocide, war, inhumanity and evil... In just one hundred days, over 800,000 innocent Rwandan men, women and children were brutally murdered while the developed world, impassive and apparently unperturbed, sat back and watched the unfolding apocalypse or simply changed channels.[3]

A little further on in the book, he declares,

> What I have come to realize as the root of it all… is
> the fundamental indifference of the world commu-
> nity to the plight of seven to eight million black Af-
> ricans in a tiny country that had no strategic or re-
> source value to any world power. An overpopulated
> little country that turned in on itself and destroyed
> its own people, as the world watched and yet could
> not manage to find the political will to intervene.
> Engraved still in my brain is the judgment of a small
> group of bureaucrats who came to "assess" the situ-
> ation in the first weeks of the genocide: "We will
> recommend to our government not to intervene as
> the risks are high and all that is here are humans."[4]

In this instance, the West was content to watch a small country, populated by people with a different colour skin, self-
destruct because it had no "resources of value" – *other than
people!*

Similar dynamics play themselves out in other countries
all over the world, though often it is the *presence* of those resources of value that lies at the centre of the conflict.

During the first week of April 2001, I was part of a church leaders' exposure tour of Southern Sudan. We visited the areas hardest hit by the ongoing civil war just south of the oil fields, and met with the most vulnerable people, as well as with local officials and church leaders.

The civil war had been going on since 1983, killing two million people and displacing more than four million. Although there were (and still are) many conflicting parties, the major conflict was between the Sudanese government in the north and the people of the south, where there are extensive oil fields. Part of our mandate was to explore the relationship between the oil companies (including Canadian companies), the military, the government, and the slaughter of innocent people.

We travelled as far into the bush as possible to see the conditions and to meet people on the run. We were particularly moved by the stories told to us by people who, in terror, had fled their defenceless villages, which were being attacked by government troops and by government-supported militias. These people had been forced to leave behind their dead and injured relatives, including women, children, and the elderly.

There was no doubt that the rapid development and production of oil in the southern region was a major factor in the suffering of these millions of innocent people. Oil reserves funded the regime's war machine. Therefore, the oil companies, including a Canadian one, were also implicated in the horror.

Our trip was an excruciating lesson in the intimate connection between military governments, foreign extraction industries, poor people, religious differences, social tensions, globalization, and human rights violations. The war in Southern Sudan – inextricably related to the development of lucrative oil fields (which function to make money for Western shareholders) – exposed the ugly underbelly of all the ethical issues of corporate social responsibility (CSR). (Thankfully, many transnational corporations are seeking ways to exercise CSR more transparently and effectively. Still, there is a long way to go.)

The story of the Dalits, the poor indigenous people of India, provides yet another case in point. The Dalits experience the negative forces of globalization more than most. Huge so-called "development" projects, such as dams, force these peasants off their lands. The caste system, the unjust exercise of power, and a lack of adequate jobs to replace even what their subsistence farming brought them, only serve to increase their poverty and the economic injustices they face.

These projects illustrate the connection between ecological damage and poverty. Routinely, people like the Dalits in India (and the Lubicon in Canada, whom I wrote about in Chapter 3) bear the costs of so-called progress, and, just as routinely, they are excluded from the benefits.

Interrelation and integration

The point is that issues of health, economic justice, poverty, ecology, education, racism, sexism, patriarchy, trade, globalization, peace, war, and housing are so interrelated in the 21st century that none of them (and others I haven't mentioned) can be dealt with in isolation.

This is why a New Story that integrates all of life's dimensions is so necessary.

Thankfully, many individuals and organizations have begun initiatives that seek to provide an integrating lens through which to address our most pressing concerns. They include Raffi Cavoukian's "Child Honouring Covenant" and related principles, "The Earth Charter," "The Canadian Index of Wellbeing," and the "Faith and the Common Good" network.

Child Honouring

I already mentioned Raffi Cavoukian's "Child Honoring" initiative in Chapter 1. To reiterate what I said there, "child honouring" is an innovative and integrating lens through which to see the world and make decisions. Will our decisions improve the lives of the 20 percent of Canadian children (or almost 25 percent of American children) who live in severe poverty? And what about the untold millions of children living in poverty around the globe? Will our decisions ensure the best possible education for all children, regardless of their parent's economic situation? Will our decisions ensure that children, no matter where they live, are not poisoned or infected with preventable diseases? If we asked of every public policy decision how it will affect children, the quality of our decision-making might improve greatly. Let the effects of public policy on children be our guide.

The Canadian Index of Wellbeing

The Canadian Index of Wellbeing is a sophisticated instrument designed to measure the health of our society as a whole. As such, it is vastly superior to the Gross Domestic Product (GDP), which only measures money. Whenever money is spent, the GDP goes up. This means that natural or human-made disasters register as a positive on the GDP, because money is spent on cleanup, insurance, reconstruction, relief services, and the like. If a corporation makes money by clear-cutting a forest, their activity has a positive effect on the GDP, even if the results are disastrous for the ecosystem.

If we engage in activities that destroy our ecosystems, in the long run we will destroy our economy, despite any short-term financial gains we may realize. In ethical terms, economic justice and the alleviation of poverty can not be accomplished by environmental degradation. Those who would have us believe we must choose between "jobs or the environment" are presenting a false dichotomy. Social justice and eco-justice are not conflicting goals; they are inter-related parts of the whole. If we want our grandchildren to inherit a healthy planet *and* a healthy economy, we need to live our lives and see our world holistically.

The Canadian Index of Wellbeing (CIW) is a joint project of the Atkinson Charitable Foundation and the Genuine Progress Index. It will measure such things as living standards, human health, ecosystem health, community vitality, time use, education, and civic engagement. Therefore, such things as illiteracy, pollution, and disease are counted as negative; while community involvement, disease prevention, and voluntary activity are counted as positive. The CIW is one of the new ways we are beginning to appreciate the wholeness of life. And, as it becomes linked to parallel projects around the world, it will ensure that we look at these issues in their global context using comparable international measures.

Faith and the Common Good

Faith and the Common Good (FCG) is a national interfaith initiative that seeks to address important issues of social ethics through education and action.

The origins of the FCG go back to when I was Moderator of the United Church. At that time, I chose as a focus economic justice and the prophetic role of the church in addressing issues of human deprivation. With substantial funding from the Atkinson Charitable Foundation in Toronto, we created the Moderator's Consultation on Faith and the Economy. With executive director leadership from Mike Quiggin and Dr. Ted Reeve, we produced more than 40 papers, a book, and hosted eight town hall forums, from Cape Breton, Nova Scotia; to Port Alberni, British Columbia; each of which was taped and televised.

Near the end of my term, we held a day-long symposium in the Railway Committee Room of the Parliament buildings in Ottawa. Attended by more than 200 people, the symposium included social activists, analysts, interfaith leaders, concerned citizens, and Members of Parliament from all political parties, and was televised on the parliamentary channel. Thanks to key organizers such as Gary Sealy, David MacDonald and Ted Reeve, the symposium created quite a buzz. With wonderful encouragement from Charles Pascal and the Atkinson Charitable Foundation, we created Faith and the Common Good as a follow-up to the Faith and Economy success.

A major premise of FCG is that the social ethics of the religious traditions of the world contain many profound similarities. We may disagree when it comes to our theology or doctrines, but most traditions seek peace, justice, harmony, respect, and wholeness in their social ethics.

The FCG network includes chapters in Ottawa, Toronto, Winnipeg, Calgary, and Vancouver. Dr. Ted Reeve is the executive director. Besides the funding received from the Atkinson Foundation, the FCG also receives (or received) financial support from such groups as the Toronto Atmospheric Fund, the Federal Government's One Tonne Challenge program (cancelled under the Harper government), and the Calgary Foundation.

FCG has produced television programs and materials for education and action on consumerism, health care, and ecology. Teaming up with the Suzuki Foundation, we initiated "Renewing the Sacred Balance" and "Greening Sacred Spaces." These projects inspire congregations to do environmental audits on their places of worship, and encourage them to install state-of-the art light bulbs, toilets, windows, etc. This leads to similar exploration in people's own homes and communities.

In all of this work, to truly involve many different faith traditions is a huge challenge. Yet I believe that the public expression of religious social consciousness, and any resulting action – a long tradition in Canada – is far more relevant and effective when done cooperatively among the various faith traditions. Our shared social ethics understand the issues we face holistically, within the context of Divine will. From our interfaith perspective, we understand that personal, social, and ecological justice relate to each other as part of the whole, and all of it begs wise, informed, and effective political action.

The key to our future

In his book *Free World*, Timothy Garton Ash puts all this in an interesting way. He asks, "What is the widest political community of which you spontaneously say 'we' or 'us'? I suggest we not answer too quickly. In our answer lies the key to our future."

Discussion Questions

1. How do you think a New Story can help us see and act more holistically?

2. Can you see the connection between economic justice and ecological integrity in your own environment; in your own town or city, province or state?

3. For you, what are the most helpful "lenses" through which we will be able to see and act for positive change?

4. What do you think of Kahlil Gibran's ideas on commerce?

5. What do you think of Raffi Cavoukian's "Child Honouring" lens? What new possibilities does it offer?

---

1 Dieter Hessel and Larry Rasmussen (eds) *Earth Habitat: Eco-Injustice and the Church's Response* (Minneapolis, MN: Fortress Press, 2001), 23.

2 Kahlil Gibran, *The Prophet* (New York: Alfred A. Knopf, 1991), 37.

3 Romeo Dallaire, *Shake Hands with the Devil* (Random House, 2003), xviii.

4 Ibid., 6.

6. Spirituality, Theology, Faith and Disestablishment

It is entirely natural and appropriate at a crossroads mo-ment to ask ourselves the big questions – questions about our core beliefs and values. Considering the all-encompass-ing nature of the crisis we face, one of the questions we might ask is, "What are human beings for?" Another ques-tion might be, "What is our relationship to the Earth, and to the universe?" These are spiritual questions because they involve all of life and its purpose. Humankind has a deep and intrinsic spiritual yearning, a desire to understand, to seek meaning, and to connect with the origins of life, espe-cially during challenging times.

In times past, these spiritual yearnings found expression in religion. Religion provided meaning, community, ritual, doctrine, and discipline. It formalized and organized humanity's spiritual experiences, yearnings, and questions into sets of beliefs. Almost inevitably, as these beliefs became ever more structured and formal, the question of truth arose, particularly in respect to other religious traditions. Some religious traditions began to proclaim that they alone possessed the "Truth," that their way was the *only* way to God. Of course not everyone within these religious traditions held such exclusivist views. Within each religion, there have always been, and always are, those who hold their beliefs quite rigidly, and those who recognize that their beliefs can and perhaps *should* change with time and experience, with exposure to different insights and ways of being.

Religion at the crossroads

Like everything else today, religion stands at its own crossroads as it tries to discern its role in the decisions humanity faces. I am part of a religious tradition with a rich history of exploring the nature of life, community, and the divine. Even so, my tradition has a very mixed record when it comes to the enhancement or degradation of life in all its forms. No religious tradition is perfect, and, I believe, none has a corner on the "Truth."

I believe that there are many ways to know and experience the Holy. Which is I why I believe that religion and spirituality have a crucial role to play, now more than ever. At this global crossroads, I believe that *all* religious traditions need to step forward with their insights. I believe that *all* religious traditions have profound wisdom to contribute to the spiritual quest, to humanity's understanding of the nature and purpose of life.

In order to make this contribution, though, we need to come out from behind our walls of doctrine and dogma, our rituals of worship and practice (valuable as they are), to rediscover our spiritual roots. When we do this, we will discover amazing common ground, which is necessary for the common good of the Earth and all its creatures.

My own faith

Now a word about my own faith, so it is clear where I stand in relation to my own Christian tradition.

I believe that there is a creative energy at the heart of the universe, giving purpose and direction to life. From the beginning of human consciousness, people have experienced this holy power and have sought to understand it. Thus, the world is blessed with a kaleidoscope of spiritual traditions. I believe that each tradition is rich in its own way, giving shape, intellectual substance, sustenance, and celebration to its people.

The Christian tradition, of which I am a part, is an offshoot of Judaism. Jesus was a Torah-abiding Jew, as were his parents and his first followers. For me, the Hebrew stories of the Exodus and the Exile are essential to my understanding of our relationship to God, the name we give the divine power. I believe the prophetic tradition in the Hebrew texts is essential to comprehending Jesus and his ministry.

God

I believe that God is mystery. Any name we give to God or image we use to describe God must be metaphor, for God is truly both hidden and revealed. The Bible uses a myriad of images to describe God. God is rock, wind, mother, eagle, hen, river, and yes, father. I believe that the essence of God, the heart of the universe and of the ongoing evolutionary story, is love. Without love at the centre of life, Earth would die.

Jesus

Who is Jesus? Here is Marcus Borg's 170-word statement:

> Jesus was a peasant, which tells you about his social class. Clearly, he was brilliant. His use of language was remarkable and poetic, filled with images and stories. He had a metaphoric mind. He was not ascetic: he was world affirming, with a zest for life. There was a socio-political passion to him – like a Gandhi or a Martin Luther King, he challenged the domination systems of his day. He was a religious ecstatic, a Jewish mystic if you will, for whom God was an experiential reality. As such, Jesus was also a healer. And there seems to have been a spiritual presence around him, like that reported of St. Francis or the present Dalai

Lama. And I suggest that as a figure of history, Jesus was an ambiguous figure – you could experience him and conclude that he was insane, as his family did, or that he was simply eccentric or that he was a dangerous threat – or you could conclude that he was filled with the Spirit of God.[1]

I believe that in Jesus, we glimpse as much of the nature and will of God as can be embodied in a human being. Or, as William Sloan Coffin states so well, "What is finally important is not that Christ is Godlike, but that God is Christ-like. God is life."[2]

But Jesus, as I said when I was moderator, is not the whole enchilada. I do not believe that Jesus is divine, any more than any other human being is divine. Jesus is not God. Jesus is one among many revelations of God's nature and purpose.

I do not believe that Jesus died *for* our sins. Jesus was not a sacrifice by God for the sins of the world. God is not a monster. Rather, Jesus died as a *consequence* of human sin. I believe Jesus shows us the way of love, relationship, peace, justice, and reconciliation with all from which we are alienated.

The Holy Spirit

I believe that the Holy Spirit – symbolized in the Bible by wind, fire, and breath – is the ongoing power, comfort, and presence of God in the world. The Spirit moves us, empowers us, comforts us, and opens us to new insights.

Descriptive language

You may notice that I have used the traditional Trinitarian expression of the Holy. I intend this as *descriptive* language, not *prescriptive* language. I do not believe in dogmatic or doctrinal formulae that express faith in exclusive terms. As I've said, each faith tradition has its own way of understanding love and the Holy, that Sacred Source which is revealed in the universe. (Many scientists see the holy in the wonder of evolution, in the mystery of molecules, the miraculous community of particles which give life and coherence to creation.)

Sin

I believe there is a power of sin in the world. There are evil forces that humble us, even as we seek to find solutions to the horrendous problems we face. Just as we never fully comprehend the reality of love and of forgiveness, we never fully understand the nature of evil.

Evil is elusive yet powerful. I believe these evil realities lie both deeper than and beyond our specific wrongdoing or sin. They are manifest when our good intentions result in bad or undesired outcomes. We ignore this fact at our peril. Ignoring evil feeds our arrogance. It reinforces our self-importance and the notion that we can solve all problems with the right information or with state-of-the-art technologies.

I remember William Sloane Coffin once saying that the "Assurance of Pardon" in Protestant Christian worship is the central and most important point in the whole service. And it is the one ingredient that few people believe. I agree with him. I have come to call this part of the liturgy, which follows the "Confession of Sin," the "Forgiveness and Freedom." Basically, it declares that God forgives, accepts, and frees us to be the people we were created to be. Despite our weakness, vulnerability, arrogance, and wrongdoing, God's unconditional love prevails. God understands that we make mistakes, have narrow understandings, are fragile creatures, and live with all kinds of limitations. But we are also beautiful, unique, and valued beings in God's creation.

And we are constantly liberated to do justice, love tenderly, and walk humbly with God (as the prophet Micah reminds us in Micah 6:8).

Evil is real. Human error and complicity in sin is real. We are not and will never be perfect. Regardless of how hard we try, we do things we know to be wrong, unhelpful, or just plain nasty. Terrible things happen in the world, which defy analysis or clear explanation. Similarly, good people sometimes do bad things for no apparent reason. However, we need not despair. Neither are we to give up. God loves us regardless, and calls us into loving engagement with the world.

The changing face of religion in society

Because I believe all things are interconnected and are expressions of spirituality, I believe that the crossroads we face require the spiritual traditions of the world, in their own deep interconnectedness, to weave together their distinctive spiritualities into a tapestry of hope and a vision that will help us all to change direction. The good news is that this coming together of religious traditions is more possible today than ever before.

I was raised during a time and in a city where Anglican and United Church people wielded major influence. Toronto was a city of churches. Men who worshipped every Sunday at their local Protestant church exercised most of the power. Thus, no sports or entertainment events were allowed on Sunday. Sunday was the Lord's Day and there was legislation to protect it. My parents would not even allow me to throw around a baseball or to play ball hockey on the street. I liked going over to cousin Larry Dinsmore's home on Sundays because his parents let us play catch.

Back then, beer was not allowed at Maple Leaf Gardens, or at Maple Leaf Stadium (where the International League Toronto Maple Leafs played great baseball and where I sold pop). Toronto was clearly a WASP (White Anglo Saxon Protestant) city and other groups, such as Catholics and Jews, knew their lower place in the pecking order of power.

It is amazing, then, to contemplate that over the course of about 40 years Toronto became one of the most cosmopolitan cities in the world. Certainly by the 1990s, Toronto was wide open on Sundays. And every culture or nationality in the world was contributing to its special flavour. Whereas in the 1950s the United Church of Canada was opening one church per week in Canada's burgeoning suburbs – many of these surrounding Toronto – by the 1990s it was struggling to keep many of them open.

Toronto's suburbs currently bloom with new mosques, synagogues, and temples. Some United Church congregations sold their buildings to newer "ethnic" congregations, or to more evangelical denominations, and sometimes to entirely different faith traditions. Today, Toronto reflects the faith and cultural traditions of the world. I believe this is good, even though it means the once influential and even powerful United Church of Canada is now a small minority on the religious landscape, as are the Anglicans. (Because of its sheer size and various immigrant groups, the Roman Catholic Church appears to have retained or increased its power.)

The disestablishment of religion

As author and theologian Douglas Hall so clearly documents, the "disestablishment of the churches" is today unmistakable. Canadian society can no longer be called "Christian." Whereas once moderators of the United Church could easily get appointments with the prime minister, by the 1980s the prime minister's office had no clue about the leadership of the United Church and little interest in arranging meetings on issues of national concern.

I remember a telling comment made by Gregory Baum, a leader in Catholic theology and social thought, when he addressed a gathering of United Church people around 1977. We were in a "re-missioning" process to discover the future direction of mid-city Toronto congregations. Some would have to close and find new ways of being. Yet each congregation had its own special history and times of vibrant ministry. Many of the buildings were architecturally and historically valuable. It was sobering to witness the decline of these congregations.

Gregory Baum's comment was this: "The United Church congregations are in mourning for a past that is gone." He was right. The church, as we had known it, was dead or dying and we were in a state of mourning. We needed to grieve our loss of numbers, influence, power, and place in society. Then we had to struggle with the theological, pastoral, and mission questions the new situation raised, before deciding on a faithful course of action.

In many ways, this is an ongoing process, as we try to find our way as a disestablished minority. What is our contribution to the city and to wider society? Who and whose are we? What is our ministry, and how shall we use our resources in the cause of the Christian gospel?

Despite all this, I believe that our being disestablished is a good thing. Christian theology and practice have always found solid and inspiring roots in the prophetic tradition of the Older Testament and in the Jesus movement of the Newer Testament. We are at our best when we exemplify these approaches to being faithful to the God we know in Jesus.

Equally important to the theme of this book, as a disestablished minority we no longer need to feel obligated to defend the status quo, the power structures that keep the Old Story in control. We can freely ponder honestly what the God of compassion, justice, and peace would have us be and do. We can more easily be partners with other dispossessed and marginal people. In this regard, I believe we can learn from sisters and brothers who have always been effective minorities wherever they are. For example, the Mennonite, Quaker, and Jewish communities are often in the vanguard of social justice, peace, and human rights movements.

The contrast between old established power and being disestablished was on display when Pope Benedict XVI was installed. The pomp and circumstance of imperial religion was played out in magnificent pageantry by old men in amazing costumes. People love such ceremony and drama.

Yet despite the fascination of millions of people brought to St. Peter's Square through unprecedented media coverage, such displays of imperial majesty and power fail to address the deep spiritual issues of our times. The all-male hierarchy guarding outdated traditions is far removed from the struggle of women, the liberation of the dispossessed, and the biblical experience and tradition of prophetic movements not beholden to the power brokers.

I believe we need to get out from under the antiquated structural overlays of religion so that a new spiritual energy can breathe and blossom. By this I do not mean that we should or need to abandon tradition, which frees and provides substance for our witness to justice, peace, and love. But we *do* need to relieve ourselves of religious structures that have outlasted their creative energy and serve only to protect dying institutions and irrelevant authority.

My journey of transformation

Author Burton Mack wrote that during the first century after Jesus, followers experienced an "explosion of imagination" that gave birth to a new social vision. In some ways that is what happened to me in my own faith journey.

It wasn't until I worked in Brooklyn, in 1964, that I witnessed the social justice dimension of the Christian faith. No one had told me about the Social Gospel tradition of the United Church of Canada, expressed in the ministry of such people as Salem Bland, J. S. Woodsworth, R. B. Y. Scott, and their fellow travellers. I knew nothing of the church's history of pursuing social justice for the poor, for immigrants, and for people of colour; nor of its requirement that we lobby governments and challenge oppressive corporate powers. So that summer in New York opened doors for me that have never closed.

After completing my LL.B. degree at Osgoode Hall Law School in 1965, I went to McCormick Theological Seminary in Chicago, at the encouragement of the ministers in Brooklyn, and people such as Reverend Bill Berry, in Toronto. McCormick emphasized urban ministry, which is what I wanted to explore. I attended on a full international scholarship to try it out for a year. I stayed the three years, graduating in June 1968 on the day that Bobby Kennedy was assassinated.

Part of my motivation was to see if the church could be part of social change. Even though both law and religion too often protect the powerful and the status quo, they can also initiate change on behalf of the oppressed. In the mid-1960s, Chicago was a cauldron of social activism address-ing the big three issues of the time: racism, poverty, and the Vietnam War. I saw the church in the middle of that struggle.

The seminary required "field work" as a complement to its academic curriculum. I took full advantage of the opportunities. I worked on the midnight shift at a Sun-beam Electric factory producing electric lawn mowers, as part of a program where participants reflected upon their work experience. We learned about industrial rela-tions, theological ethics, racism, city government, and of course, the realities of the factory floor.

I remember thinking that the midnight shift was best because there were fewer supervisors to give you a hard time. I recall racial tensions, when African Americans were referred to as "burr heads," and people ate lunches in segregated groups. I also recall appreciating that certain bars were open at 9:00 a.m. so that workers on the midnight shift could enjoy a cold beer after a night of hot and dirty factory work.

At the time, Saul Alinsky was the dean of community organizers and I worked for one of his organizations. His staff taught the tough realities of organizing racially-changing neighbourhoods to achieve their goals, in the course of which they fought city hall and real estate "block busters." It was hard-nosed, on the street, block-by-block organizing for democratic social change.

At the same time, I was a chaplain on the leukemia ward of Children's Memorial Hospital. Here I witnessed the uncommon courage of children and their parents, and I learned and experienced the personal pain of watching children die.

These two experiences in particular – working in the streets of racially tense neighbourhoods and being a chaplain in a children's hospital – thrust me into the reality of the prophetic/pastoral role of the church. I have tried always to honour that balance.

One particular story comes to mind. In my community organizing role, I attended a particularly difficult community meeting one evening. It concerned real estate block busters, who convinced whites to sell their homes at low prices by encouraging and exploiting a common white fear that the neighbourhood would turn "black." This fear caused them to take whatever price they could get. The realtors would then turn around and sell the same property at greatly inflated prices to a black family anxious to "move up." It was not pretty.

When I returned to my residence that evening, I received a phone call from the children's hospital saying that a young girl named Lisa was dying. So, at 2:00 a.m., I walked over to the hospital to spend time with Lisa and her parents in the last hours of her life.

Both of these types of ministries are part of living out Christian faith.

In the course of my three years at McCormick in Chicago, I also worked at St. Leonard's House, a halfway house for ex-convicts; I marched with Martin Luther King Jr. and heard him preach; I worked on Senator Eugene McCarthy's primary campaign for president; I organized a seminary emergency response program for the South Side, which blew up in riots and flames when Martin Luther King Jr. was killed; and I visited a friend in New Orleans (I had worked with her in Brooklyn in 1964), where I saw racism even more personally. In short, I saw the church fully engaged in the issues of the day, and developed a biblically-based theology and social ethics to support social justice work. Among many theologians, the work of Paul Tillich and Dietrich Bonhoeffer influenced me most.

To this day, I have kept in touch with three important friends from that period of my life. One of them, Mike Quiggin, invited me to join him at Chapel in the Park United Church, in Thorncliffe Park, a high rise community of 25,000 people in Toronto. Again, I was involved in community organizing around issues that people identified. Under the name Community Consultant Services, and funded by the United Church, we expanded our work to Rexdale and to the Lakeshore in the west end of Toronto.

When we left "the Chapel," I hooked up with a friend from the Bar Admission course, Harvin Pitch, to operate a poverty law storefront. This evolved into a community organization called "People and Law." Once again I was doing social justice work, this time as a poverty law lawyer.

When I became minister of Trinity United Church in downtown Toronto, I was told that I would be their last minister unless something changed. Over the first three or four years, we filled the church building with social justice groups. At one point, I was supervising three social work students and three theology students to help the church become a centre for community development. We became part of a mid-city "Re-Vision" project staffed by Jim Houston, a former Jesuit priest.

Trinity United Church and St. Paul's Avenue Road United Church (where I had also worked) amalgamated and became a centre for faith, justice, and the arts, a story I will tell in Chapter 8. During this time, I was deeply influenced by the emerging feminist theology, and by Liberation theology from Central America.

When I moved to Alberta in 1983, I began to learn about the long struggle for justice of First Nations peoples, and about aboriginal spirituality. Through travels in the North, and the Lubicon Cree struggle, I met wonderful people who taught me about the colonial history of Canada and about the staying power of First Nations spirituality. As moderator, I was deeply involved in the tragedy of the residential schools, the United Church response by way of apologies, the Healing Fund, and First Nations governance.

More recently, I have become convinced that interfaith action is one of the indispensable pieces of both creating and living the New Story. As I said earlier in this chapter, I believe that all faith traditions are called to share their wisdom and to offer a coherent spiritual heart to the struggles facing the Earth and all life. I believe faith is not a system of belief exclusive to one's own tradition, but a way of living. As a Christian, I believed I am not so much called to believe *in* Jesus, but to follow him.

Broadened horizons

I rehearse my own faith development in order to illustrate its growing inclusiveness, its social justice focus, and its integration of insights and experiences that deepen and broaden the confines of Christian doctrine – a spiritual transformation that in itself *embodies* the New Story and at the same time *opened* me to it.

Some of the wisdom from this broadened horizon can enlighten and encourage us.

We can reject everything else: religion,
ideology, all received wisdom.
But we cannot escape the necessity of love
and compassion.
This, then, is my true religion, my simple faith...
Our own heart, our own mind is the temple.
The doctrine is compassion.

~ DALAI LAMA IN *ETHICS FOR THE NEW MILLENNIUM*[3]

Sunyata means the complete interrelatedness
of all beings,
and *karuna* or compassion flows from this
intuition of interrelatedness.
Together, they comprise the heart of
Buddha's teaching.

~ MATTHEW FOX, *ONE RIVER, MANY WELLS*[4]

From the Veda, root scriptures of Hinduism, comes the
Shanti Mantra (mantra of peace):

> To the heavens be peace, to the sky and Earth,
>
> To the waters be peace, to all plants and trees
>
> To the gods be peace, to Brahman be peace,
>
> To all people be peace, again and again
>
> – peace also to me.

Discussion Questions

1. Write your own spiritual or faith autobiography.
2. What significant "ah-ha" experiences or turning points have you had in your faith journey?
3. How do you understand the divine, or God?
4. How do you understand the central human figure in your religious tradition?
5. How has your faith changed over the years?
6. How do you understand evil, sin, salvation, and other key concepts in religious traditions?
7. How important do you think interfaith dialogue and action are?

---

1 Marcus Borg, ed., *Jesus at 2000* (Boulder, CO: Westview Press, 1998), 10.

2 William Sloan Coffin, *Credo* (Louisville, KY: Westminster John Knox, 2005), 12.

3 As quoted in Matthew Fox, *One River, Many Wells: Wisdom Springing from Global Faiths* (New York: Jeremy P. Tarcher/Penguin, 2004), 377.

4 Ibid., 379.

7. Water

I include a chapter on water for a number of reasons. Water is central in all the concerns of this book because water is essential for all life. Water is tangible, necessary, and can't be ignored if we are to survive. Water quality is also under stress throughout the world. Water is at the forefront of ecological health, economic justice, public policy, and globalization issues.

Water knows no boundaries. It is universal and ubiquitous. The water I drink in Calgary may have washed a Buddhist prayer bowl in Tibet. The water upon which I paddle in Algonquin Park, in Ontario; or in Prince Albert Nation-

*"The more you under-
stand water, the more
difficult you will find it
to deny the existence of a
God."*

MASAU EMOTO,
THE HIDDEN MESSAGE IN WATER

*"The global fresh water
crisis looms as perhaps
the greatest threat ever
to the survival of our
planet."*

MAUDE BARLOW AND TONY CLARK,
BLUE GOLD

*"The global fresh water
supply is a shared legacy,
a public trust and a fun-
damental human right,
and therefore, a collective
responsibility."*

WATER SUMMIT FOR PEOPLE
AND NATURE, JULY 9, 2001,
BLUE GOLD

al Park, in Saskatchewan; may also have tumbled over Victoria Falls in Zimbabwe, Africa. Water quenches thirst, enables agriculture, and powers industry.

Water also has spiritual significance and is a symbol used in many spiritual traditions. We are who we are because of water. Water is life. Without it we die. When we begin life as a fetus, we are 99 percent water. When we are born, we are 90 percent water. In adulthood, we are 70 percent. We exist mostly as water. Whether or not we are aware of it, our lives are fundamentally defined and shaped by what water is and does. It is life-blood and mystery. This single substance makes our world unique, and in a deeply spiritual way, we are never separated from water. It is our most intimate companion in life's journey.

Water in the Bible and in theology

Every culture on Earth has its water stories. In the Bible, there are two (among many) striking stories about water. In one, Moses leads the Israelites on a 40-year journey through the desert. Understandably, the people complain, whine, and cause no end of grief for the man who freed them from slavery. At one point, the people are thirsty and Moses, being a man of the desert, knows what to do. He strikes a rock and *voila!* Water flows fresh and cold bringing the people life and hope.

The other story is set at a well. Jesus and his friends have stopped there to rest. While Jesus is sitting there, a Samaritan woman (two strikes against her – women were not allowed to talk to men outside their families, and Jews considered Samaritans beneath them) comes to fill her water jug. Jesus and the woman engage in conversation. At the end of their forbidden talk, the woman asks Jesus for "living water" so that she will never again thirst.

This dramatic story is usually told to illustrate how Jesus crossed boundaries and behaved in a way totally unacceptable to the culture. It is also told to refer to Jesus himself as "living water" – as a messenger from God who brings fullness of life.

Today there other boundaries – not just racial, or cultural, or those between the sexes – we can talk about in connection to this story. For example, what about the boundary we have put between humankind and the rest of the created world, especially water? How would it change our theology to think of water as a living being, as something sacred without which we would die?

It is no accident that this illustration of Jesus crossing boundaries and revealing God's truth involved water. In the Middle East, as in all arid places, water is extremely precious. People know its true value. They treat it with utmost respect. For them, water is truly sacred.

Part of the problem with our inherited theology is that, for the most part, it understands God to be separate from us and from the world. It describes God as a being who is "above" and "beyond." In our tendency to describe God this way, we have essentially been creating God in our own image, for that is how we have understood ourselves, especially since the beginning of the age of scientific rationalism. We have thought ourselves to be detached from, above, brighter than, and more important than nature – including water.

Just as Jesus crossed boundaries that maintained systems of injustice and caused harm, so I believe we need to cross a difficult boundary here – we need to see our oneness with water, our very being intertwined with it. The sacred, divine reality moves within and among us. This realization is part of the New Story. It represents a different way of thinking and believing about God, the Earth, and our place on the Earth.

The river as teacher

Author and canoeist James Raffan invites us to celebrate the river as teacher. Rivers, says Raffan, connect not only people, but landscapes as well. They travel under a changing sky, cut through rock, erode soft river banks, race or meander past forests, plains, and tundra. He continues: "Experience teaches several ways to divine where a lake ends and a river begins. All that is required is learning to think like a river."[1] Thinking like a river means paying attention to currents, winds, depths, and seasons.

Spring is a good time of year to practise this kind of thinking, as we watch ice and snow melt to free rivers and lakes, and enjoy life-giving rains. Spring is a good time to

The Spirit of God was moving over the water."

There is a river that brings joy to the city of God.

PALM 46:4A

If there is magic on this planet, it is contained in water.

L. EISLEY

We were gentle when we were with you, like a mother taking care of her children.

1 THESSALONIANS 2:7B

In Canada's larger cities, a litre of bottled water can cost as much as 5000 times as a litre of tap water.

KAIROS AND DEVELOPMENT AND PEACE (TAP INTO IT CAMPAIGN)

The frog does not drink up the pond in which it lives.

FIRST NATIONS SAYING

think about where water comes from; where it goes; how we use this sacred gift; and how, as sister, brother, and beloved friend, its life is constantly threatened.

Ecology and access in a thirsty world

Our extreme vulnerability is startling when we recognize our total dependence on water.

Only about three percent of all water on Earth is fresh. And that fresh water is deeply threatened. All the great ice fields of the world, the source of drinking water for tens of millions of people, are disappearing. The glacier feeding the Bow River, which alone is a major source of water for one million Albertans, will only last another 30 to 50 years. Untold numbers of lakes and rivers are dead or dying because of acid rain, industrial farming, and the pollution from heavy industry. Appropriately named

Devil's Lake in North Dakota is a noxious brew of salt, arsenic, boron, mercury, nitrogen, and other chemicals, and it is about to be diverted into the Red River system, Lake Winnipeg, and beyond.

Prairie rivers are drying up. In the last century, the South Saskatchewan River has declined by 80 percent, the Old Man and Peace Rivers by 40 percent, and the Athabasca River by 30 percent.

Worldwide, 1.2 billion people have no access to clean water and thousands die every day from preventable, water-related diseases. Wetlands are nature's water *purifiers*, the most efficient water filters in creation. Yet these are disappearing too. Atlantic Canada has lost 65 percent of its wetlands, Ontario 70 percent, the Prairies 71 percent, and the Fraser River Delta 80 percent. These wetlands are being destroyed mainly by urban sprawl and factory farming.

The poisoning of water is clearly an ecological issue of urgent importance. Oren Lyons, Faith-keeper of the Turtle Clan of the Onondaga Nation of the Six Nations Confederacy, recalls the ancient yet absolutely contemporary wisdom of his people:

One of the Natural laws is that you've got to keep things pure. Especially the water. Keeping the water pure is one of the first laws of life. If you destroy the water, you destroy life. That's what I mean by common sense. Anybody can see that. All life on Mother Earth depends on pure water, yet we spill every kind of dirt and filth and poison into it.[2]

The concerns surrounding water are not just ecological. Access to water and the uses to which it is put are equally important issues. For basic needs, humans require about 50 litres of water per person per day. In the developing world, people use 25 to 30 litres; Europeans use 100 to 200 litres, while North Americans use 300 to 400 litres per person per day.

Water is a strong symbol of economic injustice and corporate power. The processes used to extract oil from the Athabasca Tar Sands, for example, require nine barrels of water to produce one barrel of oil. Coca Cola, Pepsi Cola, and Nestle are three of the largest retailers of water in the world. In the United States, 30 million plastic bottles for brand-name bottled water (which is no cleaner than Calgary tap water) are discarded per day. Ninety percent of these bottles end up in landfill sites. People pay $1.50 for one bottle when they could drink fresh water out of a tap for a fraction of a penny. You can drink 4000 glasses of tap water for the same price as one six pack of Coke. Transnational corporations salivate at the profit potential in the privatization of water.

We are rapidly losing the "common sense" and age-old practice of recognizing water as a common good, held in trust for all life. We are losing any sense of proportion, value, and ethics when we begin to treat water as a mere commodity, like cola or beer.

Dawning awareness

Why is it that we waste, pollute, disregard, and privatize something so absolutely essential to life – something of which we are a part and which is so intimately a part of us?

Thankfully, people all over the world seem to have become conscious of water. Magazines, newspapers, and television are bursting with "specials" on the state of the world's water. We can no longer take it for granted, ignore it, or wish the issue would go away.

The United Nations has designated the decade from 2005 to 2015 as an "International Decade for Action: Water for Life." The actions called for include cutting in half the number of people without access to safe drinking water, and the cessation of unsustainable uses and exploitation of water resources. Churches around the world have prepared study and action resources focused on water.

Even so, tensions continue to grow worldwide as inequitable distribution of water and the pressures toward privatization persist. People cannot and will not endure for long extravagant waste alongside severe shortages. In 1884, Mark Twain said, "Whiskey is for drinking; water is for fighting wars." Many predict that wars over water will supersede wars over oil, and much more will be at stake.

Water as spiritual nourishment

Water may be the centrepiece of major political and economic struggles, but it is also becoming more central in our spiritual lives.

Eloquent statements about water book-end the biblical story. In Genesis, the first book in the Bible, four rivers flow out of Eden to nurture life in the world beyond. In the last book, Revelation, the River of Life flows through the promised City of God to nourish the Tree of Life, whose fruits feed humankind. In between, well waters, rivers, and lakes figure prominently in the stories, myths, and spirituality of the people of faith.

In the Qu'ran it says, "By means of water, we give life to everything."

Water is extremely important for my own spiritual well-being. It restores my soul, literally. I have many memories of arriving at our family cottage or at a campground located on the shores of a lake, of getting out of the car and of feeling my body relax instantly. My soul has arrived at its Earthly, geographical home.

When I was two months old, my parents took my sister Elda and me to the family cottage at Big Cedar Point on Lake Simcoe, north of Toronto. My grandfather built the cottage in 1920, on over 150 feet of shoreline. It became the gathering place for all the generations in my family. We had three canoes, but no motor boats, a strange thing on that lake.

Water has been in my bones, soul, and heart from the beginning. When I was 12 years old my parents sent me to Kilcoo Camp on Gull Lake, south of Minden, Ontario. This area in the Haliburton region is the land of my maternal ancestors. I loved camp. As I grew, so grew the canoe and the lakes of Haliburton and Algonquin Park in importance for my sense of belonging in God's amazing creation. There is nothing like the quiet dip of a paddle in calm waters. I will never forget turning a bend through the tall reeds in the northwest corner of Algonquin Park and seeing a moose, knee deep in water. The sun was setting. It was perfectly quiet. Our three canoes rested in the stillness as we contemplated this magnificent moment, a spiritual epiphany.

One of my regrets is that, after leaving Kilcoo Camp, I stopped canoe tripping until 40 years later, when I was moderator of the United Church of Canada. Knowing how much I loved Algonquin Park, Bruce Gregersen encouraged me to come on two ten-day trips, paddling some of the same lakes I had paddled four decades before. My soul rejoiced (except during a few long portages!). I am grateful that my three children enjoy and feel at home on the water. A great thrill was giving grandchildren Michael and Kate their first canoe ride when only a few months old.

I have great memories of and a profound appreciation for the many bodies of water that have restored and inspired me – the Atlantic, Pacific, and Arctic Oceans; the Mediterranean Sea; Great Bear Lake and Great Slave Lake; the Great

Lakes, and the lakes of our national and provincial parks. Then there are the rivers: the Decho (McKenzie) River, the St. Lawrence River, the Red Deer, Columbia, Hudson, Bow, Nile, and Peace Rivers.

But paddling and camping on the Zambezi River, which separates Zambia from Zimbabwe, was unique. After the World Council of Churches meeting in Harare in 1998, Hugh McCullum organized a five-day canoe trip on the Zambezi. Imagine paddling around pods of hippos. Carolyn, my wife, was not impressed when I stood in the canoe to make the perfect picture of the great beasts. Drifting to sleep to the sounds of African wildlife was amazing. I can hear, even now, their night noises, their communication across land and water. There is no better way to appreciate creation than paddling the Earth's rivers and lakes.

Pierre Trudeau once said,

What sets a canoeing expedition apart is that it purifies you more rapidly and inescapably than any other. Travel a thousand miles by train and you are a brute. Pedal five hundred miles on a bike and you remain basically bourgeois. Paddle one hundred miles in a canoe and you are already a child of nature.[3]

While bodies of water restore my soul, deserts remind me of the importance of water in all dimensions of our lives. I will always remember camping in New Mexico and Arizona as an amazing experience. It doesn't take long to thirst for water. The colours that accentuate the stark realities of desert life create their own spiritual experience. Desert places have a way of stripping away pretence and excess. Water is never far from one's thoughts. A Hopi ring I wear depicts waves of water, a constant reminder of its importance.

Everywhere in the Middle East, one is aware of water because of its absence. No wonder water plays such a key role in the religious traditions that were birthed in the Middle East. Ritual practices reflect the spiritual nature and high regard we place on this essence of life.

Beside the still waters
my soul is restored.

All the issues at play in the Old and New Stories are present in water.

Make Prayers for the Rivers

BY CAROLYN POGUE

Make prayers for the life of the rivers
Make prayers for the creeks and the streams
Make prayers to the Holy Mystery
Make prayers for Earth Mother's dreams.

Pray for what lives in the water
Pray for what lives by the shore
Pray for whatever drinks water
Pray for all that and more.

Ask for courage to clean up the rivers
Ask for hope to heal shorelines and streams
We are the ones called to action
To restore the Earth Mother's dreams.

Fall down on your knees by the water
Fall down on the muck, sand or slate
Fall down in humility, hope and love
And pray that it's not too late.

Discussion Questions

1. What are your experiences of the essential value of water?

2. How do you treat water as sacred?

3. In what ways do you conserve water?

4. What do you think are the most crucial public policies governments can make concerning water in our society?

5. What specific and practical actions can you and your community take to insure water quality and availability for all life?

1   James Raffin, *Tumblehome: Meditations and Lore from a Canoeist's Life* (Toronto: HarperCollins Canada, 2001), 4–5.

2   Quoted in Matthew Fox, *One River, Many Wells: Wisdom Springing from Global Faiths* (New York: Jeremy P. Tarcher/Penguin, 2004), 49.

3   From a plaque at the Canadian Canoe Museum, Peterborough, Ontario.

8. The Arts

In my early years as minister at Scarboro United Church in Calgary, I was privileged to work with a music director loved by people all over the city. Marilyn Perkins was a high school teacher and director of many choirs over her lifetime. She inspired so many students that they founded a "Grad Choir" when they left high school. Marilyn's love of music and of her students touched thousands of people. She directed the massed choir that opened the 1988 Winter Olympics.

Marilyn was also a devoted member of the United Church of Canada. She was raised, in part, on the Social Gospel and believed fully that faith had everything to do with social change, politics, economics, and all the rest. We enjoyed many conversations on theology, ethics, and justice. Because of her enormous contribution to the wider community, a group of people initiated the process for Marilyn to receive the Order of Canada.

In the meantime, Marilyn received news that cancer had returned to her body after more than seven years of remission. It was a horrible shock to all of us. By the time we learned that she would receive the Order of Canada, her cancer had progressed too far for her to be able to travel to Ottawa to receive the award from Governor General Adrienne Clarkson. So we arranged for Lieutenant Governor Lois Hole of Alberta, another outstanding woman, to come to Calgary to give Marilyn the honour at a celebration at Scarboro United Church.

Lois Hole was a down-to-Earth, personable businesswoman, famous for her gardening books and her energizing zest for life. She treated each person she met with special attention.

That day, Lois delivered a thoughtful and challenging speech, not your typical speech with Lieutenant Governor-type platitudes. You have to understand that this was during a time of mean-spirited government cuts to the arts, to education, and to health care. Although Lieutenants Governor are not noted for giving "political" speeches, Lois launched into a description of how important the arts are for creating well-rounded citizens and especially for community and political leaders. She said, "If all politicians or corporate leaders sang in a choir, acted in a play, played a musical instrument, or painted watercolours, we would have a different world. And we would have far more understanding about the importance of the arts as essential to any culture, any society." Everyone was deeply saddened when Lois Hole also died of cancer only two years later.

The artist as prophet

I believe that artists – writers, composers, musicians, painters, sculptors, weavers, playwrights, actors, singers – are the real prophets of any age. The artist reflects society back to itself. The artist exposes relationships, public policies, and cultural addictions for what they are. The artist tells and reveals truth. The artist paints, writes, sings, acts, composes, sculpts and weaves the way to new insights, directions, values, and dreams. Without the artist, the human spirit would be dead. The artist judges and hopes. The artist unveils who we really are, and dreams with us who we can become. The artist as prophet exposes the Old Story, with all its ugliness and death, and at the same time points to the New Story and all its possibilities.

Hadani Ditmars is a Muslim journalist who wrote *Dancing in the No Fly Zone* based on her frequent visits to war-torn Iraq. In a review of that book, *Toronto Star* columnist Olivia Ward quoted Ditmars as saying,

> In the mist of despair I found art, beauty, architecture and music. I discovered a world of orchestras that played wonderfully with passion, symphonies on wrecked instruments, playwrights who pushed the limits of censorship, artists who spent their last *dinars* on paint and canvas, who lived for higher experience that transcended consumerist definitions of success.[1]

If we truly want to embrace a New Story, the artists in our midst will be indispensable.

One reason for this is because the arts invite us to recover a sense of awe, wonder, and mystery. Each of us can probably remember a moment in a theatre when we were literally "awestruck." Abraham Heschel, one of the most influential rabbis of the 20th century, said, "As civilization advances, the sense of wonder declines...life without wonder is not worth living. What we lack is not a will to believe, but a will to wonder." The sense of wonder is a hallmark of the human species, a characteristic of the human spirit.

I believe that both religion and the arts are called to make visible the transcendence of all life. In a way, the arts are like a candle in the darkness, taking us beyond ourselves and sustaining our hope. As Mary Grey says in her book *Sacred Longings*, we are called to "re-enchant a broken-hearted world."[2]

As I think about the arts and religion together, I invite us all to

a) examine our roles as critics and as bearers of hope – as well as of justice, dignity, and peace;

b) take seriously the call to social transformation through the arts;

c) be bold, courageous, on the edge, and prophetic;

d) create and re-tell compelling stories of compassion, non-violence, social justice, and peace and hope, and;

e) recover wonder, awe, and mystery.

In his book *Learning the Arts in an Age of Uncertainty*, Walter Pitman writes,

> Men and women in the twenty-first century will need access to the ways by which transformation is possible. Throughout the ages, great songs, poems, novels, drama and music have moved minds and hearts toward greater understanding and self-realization. They have provided the images which have impelled us to act in the best interests of ourselves and the collective. The power of the arts to rouse compassion and generosity of spirit is well recognized... The arts will be the essential path to our understanding of ourselves and the world we live in as the cultural supersedes the economic and political definitions of our humanity.[3]

Painting the way

The idea of the visual artist as prophet is as old as humankind. Old- and New-Story themes can be found in works by "professional" artists, and in neighbourhood graffiti and murals. I think of Edward Burtyznsky's dramatic photographs of factories, rusting equipment, and denuded landscapes. I also marvel at mural art in Mexico, Nicaragua, and El Salvador.

Visual artists are often brave in their depiction of life, with all its ugliness and beauty. When Carolyn and I visited New York in 2004, we went to see an exhibit of the works of Modigliani at The Jewish Museum. The show was good, but very crowded. Also at the museum was a show about Friedl Dicker-Brandeis, so we left the crowds and went upstairs. We did not know this woman, but we were curious. The show blew us away. We stood in the presence of great art, created by a great woman.

Friedl Dicker-Brandeis was a painter, teacher, and designer. She was born in Vienna, Austria, in 1898 and was murdered in Auschwitz in 1944. Besides painting, she designed furniture and created stage sets for Bertolt Brecht. She was a teacher whose theories became the foundation for art therapy. She was the life of any party.

Before her death in Auschwitz, she had been interned in the Terezin Concentration camp, where many of the children were housed. She said, "Terezin is a unique place; a piano concert on a rooftop one night and a transport to death the next day." A teacher to the end of her days, Dicker-

Brandeis scrounged and begged art supplies, and created a makeshift studio. She gave art lessons to the children, graded their work, and released their talent and laughter. She said, "If we're only given a day, we have to live it." About 5000 of the paintings and drawings done by the children were discovered after the war and are reproduced in books about Terezin. Some of the children's paintings hang in a gallery in Yad Vashem, the Holocaust Memorial Museum in Jerusalem. Shortly before her death, this amazing woman said, "I turned out more courageous than I had supposed."[4]

Music as common ground

In mid November 2004, 13 Israeli and ten Palestinian teenagers performed 11 musical concerts before 11,000 people in Kentucky. It was an astounding event. Although they lived less than two hours away from each other in their respective homelands, they had never met, nor was it possible for them to meet, until they left the Middle East. In their music on different soil, they found common ground. For those few days they lived in peace, hope, and joy as they shared their common humanity.

One of the songs they performed was John Lennon's *Imagine*. They sang it in Arabic, Hebrew, and English. Their singing together created community. From being sworn enemies who did not know each other, they became friends who could recognize their common humanity. One of the Palestinian boys said, "Joy is the weapon." This sharing of healing typifies the New Story.

Before he took his position as the new conductor of the Montreal Symphony Orchestra, Kent Nagano said, "An orchestra should be a window into the heart and soul of the community. And the community should feel that the concert hall is its home."

While I was a minister in Toronto, two idealistic young people, Ken Solway and Susan Graves, asked if they could start a baroque orchestra in our church, Trinity-St. Paul's. The acoustics in the sanctuary are excellent.

Not much was going on in the church at the time. One or two small social justice groups had offices in old Sunday school rooms, but the sanctuary, which seats 1200 people, was empty most of the week and so the church board said yes to this expression of youthful enthusiasm.

Now, 26 years later, Tafelmusik is a world-renowned baroque ensemble whose music has touched hearts everywhere. More impressively, as a group they have recognized the responsibility they share with all artists to bring about the kind of social transformation described above. And so they have performed in support of such groups as Education Wife Assault, Smile Theatre CO, Development Education Bookstore, and the Toronto Committee for the Liberation of South Africa.

Despite pressure to move to a more modern venue, Tafelmusik continues to rehearse in the sanctuary and to host an extensive season of baroque music there. In the words of the musicians, it is their "spiritual home."

No doubt due in part to the influence of Tafelmusik, Trinity-St. Paul's is today a dynamic centre for justice and the arts. I will write more about this later.

Theatre and worship

When I think of the arts, especially of theatre, and of my role as worship leader, I see numerous similarities. In many ways, the observance and practise of religious traditions is drama at its most profound level. I think particularly of the Sun Dance, the Seder meal, and the ritual of *Diwali*.

Actors and clergy have much in common. Both rely on costumes (just think of the pope's funeral); and both use symbols or props, as well as music, poetry, sacred texts, and multi-media. Both actors and clergy seek to touch the heart and the mind, and both attempt to do this before an audience or a congregation.

But that is not all. Both theatre and worship are built around a plot line, however esoteric. Basically, they both tell stories. Both exist on the margins of a secular, hyper-consumerist, anti-intellectual, security-obsessed, and market-driven society. Both are called to bear public witness to truth from the margins. Fundamentally, both theatre and worship are about transformation. Both are called to critique society and its pre-occupations, and to give glimpses of hope. These are huge responsibilities.

Some would say that good worship is good theatre and that good theatre is deeply spiritual, touching the heart and soul of what life is all about. In June 2005, I gave the theme address to the Professional Association of Canadian Theatres. Before I went to the conference, I visited a member of our congregation who was in palliative care. When I told him where I was going, his eyes lit up. In the ensuring animated conversation, we agreed that life is a spiritual drama.

Earlier in this book, I talked about how we can no longer afford to compartmentalize life. I shared this same insight with the people at the conference. In particular, I told them that I went into ministry in the 1960s because I saw the church as a major instrument of social change.

I also told them about my summer as a young student in New York City, where I experienced profoundly the role of theatre in bringing transformation about. Plays such as *The Blacks, After the Fall* and other off-Broadway productions changed my life.

Neither the church nor the theatre, I suggested to the conference, exists for itself. Both exist for the sake of the world, for its healing and for its transformation. They are not elite clubs seeking to protect their members from life.

The gift of the writer and of the filmmaker

Throughout history, writers have played a key role by pricking the conscience of the dominant culture – a fact that is no less true today than it ever was. When I think of contemporary writers and of books they have written that have challenged the Old Story, my mind immediately turns to Margaret Atwood's *Oryx and Crake*, Doris Lessing's *Mara and Dann*, and Richard Wright's *Scientific Romance*. All three writers present very different, well-told stories set in the aftermath of ecological disaster. Of course, one could name a great many other writers – working in various genres – who are taking up the theme of social transformation.

Since its invention, film has been a superb artistic vehicle for contrasting the Old and the New Story. I think in particular of films such as *Jesus of Montreal; Romero; Good Night, and Good Luck; Brokeback Mountain; Crash; Syriana; Modern Times; The End of Suburbia;* and *The Corporation*.

Spirituality, faith, justice, and the arts

In a wonderful book called *One River, Many Wells*, Matthew Fox reflects on the importance of the arts in "writing" a New Story. He says,

> The Spirit is more at work today than ever precisely because our species is at such a moral and survival crossroads. Artists of all kinds are needed today to let "art for art's sake" ideologies go and learn to

serve the community anew with truth telling. This truth telling must be about the beauty of our existence and about the ugliness and evil that confront us and in which we participate.[5]

To conclude this chapter, I want to mention an exciting development taking shape across North America, and undoubtedly elsewhere as well. I am referring to the emergence of communities of faith who are consciously trying to bring together spirituality, faith, justice, and the arts. The church I served in Brooklyn over 40 years ago is part of this trend. Lafayette Avenue Presbyterian Church has long reached out to marginalized people, and been a home to various artistic groups. Lafayette seeks to more intentionally express these relationships in their public presence.

Trinity-St. Paul's United Church, in Toronto, mentioned earlier in regard to Tafelmusik, seeks to find formal, contractual ways for arts, justice, and congregational life to exist and work together. They do this through an organized "Centre for Faith, Justice and the Arts." Arts groups, social justice organizations, and the congregation have all been sharing one building for almost three decades now. Key to this development has been the ability of each group to take the significant next step of seeing itself as a partner in a larger enterprise.

Scarboro United Church in Calgary, from which I retired in 2007, started ScarboroArts, an initiative growing out of the fact that the church building is home to a variety of musical organizations, including children's choirs, the Westside Seniors Choir, the Foothills Brass, the Renaissance Singers, and the Bach Society, to name a few. This self-conscious process is in its early stages.

I believe there is a natural and intricate relationship between spirituality, faith, justice-seeking, peace-building, and artistic expressions of all kinds. My dream is that those engaged in all these contributions to the common good will recognize their synergy and form dynamic networks to give expression to the New Story. Just imagine the possibilities.

Discussion Questions

1. Why do you think the arts are considered "fringe" activities?

2. How important are the arts to you?

3. Do you agree that artists are the prophets of any given age?

4. If so, how can artists and their work be better understood, recognized, and celebrated?

5. How can the arts be made more central in education and beyond?

6. How can the arts be funded better, and freed from gambling and lottery revenue?

1 Olivia Ward, "Finding Dignity Amid the Chaos," in *The Toronto Star*, May 22, 2005, D6.

2 Mary Grey, *Sacred Longings: The Ecological Spirit and Global Culture* (Minneapolis: Fortress Press, 2004), 86.

3 Walter Pitman, *Learning the Arts in an Age of Uncertainty* (Toronto: Arts Education Council of Ontario, 1998), 190–191

4 Elena Makarova and Regina Seidman-Miller, *Friedl Dicker-Brandeis: Vienna 1898 – Auschwitz 1944* (Los Angeles: Tallfellow Press, 1999).

5 Matthew Fox, *One River, Many Wells: Wisdom Springing from Global Faiths* (New York: Jeremy P. Tarcher/Penguin, 2004), 430.

9. Humility

In 1985, I participated in a wonderful experiential education program organized by Father René Fumoleau and the Dene Cultural Institute in the Northwest Territories. The goal of this "Denendeh Seminar" was to expose Dene (aboriginal peoples of the NWT or "Denendeh") cultures to non-native people from the southern provinces. As a recently arrived, middle-aged, well-educated (by Western standards) white guy from Toronto, then Edmonton, it was a marvellous, mind-blowing experience.

I lived many stories during those ten days. Among them was witnessing the Dene Assembly in session at Deline (then known as Fort Franklin). Another involved a one-day fast. We were taken by boat across Great Bear Lake, from Deline to the opposite shore. We had sleeping bags, but no tents. We did not have any food or water. We were told to spread out on the tundra, out of sight and sound of each other, and to be totally alone for 24 hours.

As I gazed over the flat, endless tundra of the North, all I saw was a brownish grey wasteland. Wilderness. Nothing there. It was only when I dropped to my knees and looked closely at the ground that I saw the delicately-coloured flowers, the multi-shaded mosses, the crawling insects, a bird's nest. The tundra was literally teeming with life. But it was only when I knelt in an attitude of prayer that I realized where I was.

The whole experience humbled me, challenged my assumptions, put me in a new place. Humility is the necessary centre from which we can dare to create a New Story. Humility means recognizing our small yet unique place in all creation. Humility means understanding how limited our knowledge and experience really is.

There is a short creation story I like that speaks to the necessity of humility.

One day, a group of scientists got together and decided that human beings had come a long way and no longer needed God. So they picked one scientist to go and tell God the news. The scientist walked up to the Creator and said, "God, we've decided we have reached the point where we can clone people, modify seeds, and do many miraculous things. Why don't you just go now? We don't need you."

God listened patiently and kindly to the man (and make no mistake – this *was* a *man* speaking). After the scientist finished, God said, "Very well, how about this? Let's say we have a human-making contest."

The scientist liked challenges and immediately agreed.

"But," God said, "we're going to do it like I did back in the old days, with Adam."

The scientist was eager to begin. "No problem!" he said, and bent down to grab a hand full of dirt.

The Creator sighed. "No, no, no," God said. "You go and get your own dirt."

The power of images and metaphor

Images can be very powerful. Sometimes they reveal values, priorities, our innermost selves, more than words or other experiences. Images can become metaphors for a society.

Several years ago, two images became metaphors for my understanding of who we are. They represented alternative worldviews and even, to some extent, the Old and New stories. Both overlapped on television. Both involved political leaders, but please understand that my comments below relate to their *vehicles*, not necessarily to their political careers. The *vehicles* are the metaphors, not the people. I am not making a large "P" political statement. Rather, I am suggesting a much wider meaning, which, I believe, reflects important choices we are making as a culture and as a society. The vehicles, and the choices they represent, are part of the Old and New stories.

The jet ski and the canoe

The first image is of Stockwell Day, dressed in a wetsuit, riding his "jet ski" up onto the beach for an early press conference as the new leader of the Reform/Alliance Party. (Both Stockwell Day's leadership and the Reform/Alliance party itself have since passed into the history books, but that is another story.) The other image is of former Prime Minister Pierre Trudeau, dressed in a buckskin jacket, paddling his canoe for the television series about his life. The focus of my reflection, as I said, is not on the two men, but rather on the two vehicles. .

The jet ski represents the Old Story, which has us in its wasteful grip. The jet ski is nothing but a "boy toy," with no redeeming or useful purpose. It burns gas, makes horrendous noise, carries nothing, and is only used to roar around lakes, often endangering swimmers, fish, birds, and other living things.

Mr. Day thought he was showing that he was the "man for the time" – a new, contemporary politician. Unfortunately, the jet ski *does* represent current values: specifically, the misuse of resources and the trivialization of life itself.

On the other hand, the canoe represents both an ancient story *and* the New Story. It is quiet, uses no fuel other than human energy, carries cargo, is not wasteful, disturbs no one, and reconnects the paddler with the Earth. It is both useful and recreational. The canoe was the prime mode of transportation throughout North America for millennia, connecting all parts of the continent. An examination of pre-European-contact trade patterns, which used the canoe on the intricate network of rivers, is enough to boggle the mind. Even today, the canoe is essential transportation for people and freight in many parts of the world.

As metaphors for our values and as representations of the Old and New stories, the jet ski and the canoe are opposites. The jet ski wastes resources, assaults the natural world, and feeds human greed and arrogance. The canoe conserves resources, puts one in touch with the natural world, and feeds the deeply spiritual part of human nature.

Kirk Whipper, founder of the Canadian Canoe Museum in Peterborough, Ontario, said, "The canoe teaches us that we are part of a complex web of life and that there is an interdependence between humankind and nature."[1]

Pierre Trudeau said,

A canoeing expedition... involves a starting rather than a parting. Although it assumes the breaking of ties, its purpose is not to destroy the past, but to lay a foundation for the future... And may every dip of your paddle lead you toward a discovery of yourself, of your canoeing companion, of the wonder of nature, and of the unmatched physical and spiritual rapture made possible by the humble canoe.[2]

These things can not be said about the jet ski. For me, the canoe is a powerful metaphor for the New Story, rooted in ancient stories. The jet ski is a metaphor for the Old Story, the destructive and unsustainable story we are living currently.

Overcoming our anthropocentrism

It will take genuine humility for us to overcome our extreme anthropocentricism. But unless we do, we will never learn our rightful place *in* nature. Humankind is not the end or pinnacle of creation, as the creation story above reminds us. Nor are we masters of nature destined to conquer it for our own short-sighted purposes – an idea the jet ski seems to embody. Creation is far more mysterious and far bigger than any religious or scientific explanation. Our creation stories and cultural narratives are myths that tell us some of the story, but not all of it.

Humility will allow us to appreciate our humble place in the wondrous whole in which we will find our true destiny. One of the great contributions of indigenous spirituality is its total understanding of the sacredness of the Earth. Indigenous peoples hold the entire Earth as sacred, not just the parts of it they like.

When we remember our vulnerability and frailty, compassion, justice, and peace become possible. When we realize that arrogance, empire, wealth, and self-righteousness prevent a new, life-giving story from taking hold, we will be on the way to a genuine universal salvation.

The last shall be first, and the weak shall be strong

In the Christian tradition, Jesus did *not* come to rescue a few "saved" individuals from the clutches of an evil world. He came, according to the scriptures, for the sake of the world. In his vulnerability, Jesus showed the way to true solidarity and life abundant.

There is a simple and wonderful hymn we sing throughout the season of Advent leading up to Christmas. We sing one verse each of the four Sundays of Advent. The song is called "Hope is a Star," and it was written by Brian Wren. Each verse begins with the Advent theme for that week: Hope, Peace, Joy, and finally, Love. The refrain is, "When God is a child there's joy in our song. The last shall be first and the weak shall be strong, and none shall be afraid."

No wonder tears fill my eyes each time we sing this song; it hits the essential elements of humility so necessary in the life of faith. First, the refrain tells us that the Christmas story is about a child who reveals to us the nature and will of God. Children bring joy to our hearts. Bursting into song cannot be far behind. It also tells us that the message of Jesus results in the reversal of what we think is normal or just; that is, the first shall be last and the last shall be first.

And none shall be afraid

The promise of this humble witness is that "none shall be afraid." Fear lies at the heart of so much hubris, violence, protection, and concern for "security" in all its dehumanizing manifestations. Imagine no fear! If we could only live into this song.

Humility allows us to acknowledge our real condition and to lift the veil on the lies that encourage our fear. In his book *Finding Peace*, Jean Vanier says,

We become prophets of peace when we discover our weakness. Here we are touching mystery. Peace doesn't come from superiority and might. It comes from this power of life that flows from the deepest, most vulnerable part of our being, a power of gentle and strong life that is in you and in me.[3]

Do justice, love tenderly, walk humbly

Isaiah 58:1–12 and Micah 6:8 are ancient biblical texts from my tradition that inspire me. Micah asks what God requires of us. He answers his own question and replies in effect, "do justice, love tenderly, and walk humbly with God." Doing justice is the hard-nosed work of living in solidarity with the oppressed, whoever they are (including Earth). Loving tenderly refers to that gentle love that allows us to sit in silence while cradling a dying child, parent – or anyone – in our arms. Walking humbly with God means knowing our limitations, appreciating our rightful place in creation, and opening ourselves to the Creator's loving spirit. These teachings, joined with the inspiration of the way of Jesus and with the profound wisdom of many faith traditions, give me hope that we may write a New Story, a different narrative to guide humankind's life on Earth.

Humility also allows us to realize that we are not alone in this yearning and quest for wholeness of life throughout the Earth. Reinhold Niebuhr was one of the most articulate and influential Protestant American theologians and ethicists of the 20th century. In the 1940s and 1950s, he taught at Union Theological Seminary in New York City. In a now-famous passage, Niebuhr reminds us that

> Nothing worth doing is completed in our lifetime; therefore we must be saved by hope. Nothing true or beautiful or good makes complete sense in any immediate context of history; therefore, we must be saved by faith. Nothing we do, however virtuous, can be accomplished alone; therefore we are saved by love.

The Old and New Stories revisited

In choosing such stark contrasts of Old and New Story to frame my arguments, I may be overstating the case. Those who know me are aware that I rarely make categorical statements; rarely see events, issues, or the world in black-and-white terms. Trained as a lawyer, I tend to see many sides, multiple hues, gradations of "good and evil," "right and wrong." No story is completely a New Story and therefore "good." Neither are all Old Stories "bad" or irrelevant.

Each generation faces its own challenges and draws on ancient wisdom to write its own narrative. Perhaps Thomas Berry's phrase "the Great Work" is a better way of pointing to a viable, beautiful, and whole future. Or perhaps just "The Story" would allow more flexibility and nuances to the picture I have painted. One could talk of "life-draining or life-destroying stories," as well as of "life-giving stories." Roger Hutchinson talks of "co-existing tendencies," in the context of his outstanding teaching of Christian ethics. In fact, these observations were raised during engaging conversations with Roger and other friends, as I sought clarity and response while setting out my arguments.

With a sense of humility, I chose to stay with the metaphor of Old and New Story in order to illustrate the two poles between which creation and humankind hang precariously. However uncharacteristic of my normal form of discourse this may be, I hope it allows us to be galvanized into faithful and intelligent action before it is too late.

Discussion Questions

1. In this chapter I use the jet ski and the canoe as metaphors for the Old and New Stories. What metaphors can you come up with?
2. Is humility possible?
3. What individuals or groups do you admire for their humility, insight, and action?
4. Is humility necessary for the changes needed and, if so, how do we develop it?
5. What other essential qualities do you think are required for creating a New Story?

---

1   From a plaque at the Canadian Canoe Museum in Peterborough, Ontario.

2   Ibid.

3   Jean Vanier, *Finding Peace* (New York: Continuum International Publishing Group, 2006).

The Earth Charter:

Values and Principles for a Sustainable Future

PREAMBLE

We stand at a critical moment in Earth's history, a time when humanity must choose its future. As the world becomes increasingly interdependent and fragile, the future at once holds great peril and great promise. To move forward we must recognize that in the midst of a magnificent diversity of cultures and life forms we are one human family and one Earth community with a common destiny. We must join together to bring forth a sustainable global society founded on respect for nature, universal human rights, economic justice, and a culture of peace. Towards this end, it is imperative that we, the peoples of Earth, declare our responsibility to one another, to the greater community of life, and to future generations.

Earth, Our Home

Humanity is part of a vast evolving universe. Earth, our home, is alive with a unique community of life. The forces of nature make existence a demanding and uncertain adventure, but Earth has provided the conditions essential to life's evolution. The resilience of the community of life and the well-being of humanity depend upon preserving a healthy biosphere with all its ecological systems, a rich variety of plants and animals, fertile soils, pure waters, and clean air. The global environment with its finite resources is a common concern of all peoples. The protection of Earth's vitality, diversity, and beauty is a sacred trust.

The Global Situation

The dominant patterns of production and consumption are causing environmental devastation, the depletion of resources, and a massive extinction of species. Communities are being undermined. The benefits of development are not shared equitably and the gap between rich and poor is widening. Injustice, poverty, ignorance, and violent conflict are widespread and the cause of great suffering. An unprecedented rise in human population has overburdened ecological and social systems. The foundations of global security are threatened. These trends are perilous – but not inevitable.

The Challenges Ahead

The choice is ours: form a global partnership to care for Earth and one another or risk the destruction of ourselves and the diversity of life. Fundamental changes are needed in our values, institutions, and ways of living. We must realize that when basic needs have been met, human development is primarily about being more, not having more. We have the knowledge and technology to provide for all and to reduce our impacts on the environment. The emergence of a global civil society is creating new opportunities to build a democratic and humane world. Our environmental, economic, political, social, and spiritual challenges are interconnected, and together we can forge inclusive solutions.

Universal Responsibility

To realize these aspirations, we must decide to live with a sense of universal responsibility, identifying ourselves with the whole Earth community as well as our local communities. We are at once citizens of different nations and of one world in which the local and global are linked. Everyone shares responsibility for the present and future well-being of the human family and the larger living world. The spirit of human solidarity and kinship with all life is strengthened when we live with reverence for the mystery of being, gratitude for the gift of life, and humility regarding the human place in nature.

We urgently need a shared vision of basic values to provide an ethical foundation for the emerging world community. Therefore, together in hope we affirm the following interdependent principles for a sustainable way of life as a common standard by which the conduct of all individuals, organizations, businesses, governments, and transnational institutions is to be guided and assessed.

PRINCIPLES

I. Respect and Care for the Community of Life

1. **Respect Earth and life in all its diversity.**

a. Recognize that all beings are interdependent and every form of life has value regardless of its worth to human beings.

b. Affirm faith in the inherent dignity of all human beings and in the intellectual, artistic, ethical, and spiritual potential of humanity.

2. **Care for the community of life with understanding, compassion, and love.**

a. Accept that with the right to own, manage, and use natural resources comes the duty to prevent environmental harm and to protect the rights of people.

b. Affirm that with increased freedom, knowledge, and power comes increased responsibility to promote the common good.

3. **Build democratic societies that are just, participatory, sustainable, and peaceful.**

a. Ensure that communities at all levels guarantee human rights and fundamental freedoms and provide everyone an opportunity to realize his or her full potential.

b. Promote social and economic justice, enabling all to achieve a secure and meaningful livelihood that is ecologically responsible.

4. **Secure Earth's bounty and beauty for present and future generations.**

a. Recognize that the freedom of action of each generation is qualified by the needs of future generations.

b. Transmit to future generations values, traditions, and institutions that support the long-term flourishing of Earth's human and ecological communities.

In order to fulfill these four broad commitments, it is necessary to: ·

II. Ecological Integrity

5. **Protect and restore the integrity of Earth's ecological systems, with special concern for biological diversity and the natural processes that sustain life.**

a. Adopt at all levels sustainable development plans and regulations that make environmental conservation and rehabilitation integral to all development initiatives.

b. Establish and safeguard viable nature and biosphere reserves, including wild lands and marine areas, to protect Earth's life support systems, maintain biodiversity, and preserve our natural heritage.

c. Promote the recovery of endangered species and ecosystems.

d. Control and eradicate non-native or genetically modified organisms harmful to native species and the environment, and prevent introduction of such harmful organisms.

e. Manage the use of renewable resources such as water, soil, forest products, and marine life in ways that do not exceed rates of regeneration and that protect the health of ecosystems.

f. Manage the extraction and use of non-renewable resources such as minerals and fossil fuels in ways that minimize depletion and cause no serious environmental damage.

6. **Prevent harm as the best method of environmental protection and, when knowledge is limited, apply a precautionary approach.**

a. Take action to avoid the possibility of serious or irreversible environmental harm even when scientific knowledge is incomplete or inconclusive.

b. Place the burden of proof on those who argue that a proposed activity will not cause significant harm, and make the responsible parties liable for environmental harm.

c. Ensure that decision making addresses the cumulative, long-term, indirect, long distance, and global consequences of human activities.

d. Prevent pollution of any part of the environment and allow no build-up of radioactive, toxic, or other hazardous substances.

e. Avoid military activities damaging to the environment.

7. **Adopt patterns of production, consumption, and reproduction that safeguard Earth's regenerative capacities, human rights, and community well-being.**

a. Reduce, reuse, and recycle the materials used in production and consumption systems, and ensure that residual waste can be assimilated by ecological systems.

b. Act with restraint and efficiency when using energy, and rely increasingly on renewable energy sources such as solar and wind.

c. Promote the development, adoption, and equitable transfer of environmentally sound technologies.

d. Internalize the full environmental and social costs of goods and services in the selling price, and enable consumers to identify products that meet the highest social and environmental standards.

e. Ensure universal access to health care that fosters reproductive health and responsible reproduction.

f. Adopt lifestyles that emphasize the quality of life and material sufficiency in a finite world.

8. **Advance the study of ecological sustainability and promote the open exchange and wide application of the knowledge acquired.**

a. Support international scientific and technical cooperation on sustainability, with special attention to the needs of developing nations.

b. Recognize and preserve the traditional knowledge and spiritual wisdom in all cultures that contribute to environmental protection and human well-being.

c. Ensure that information of vital importance to human health and environmental protection, including genetic information, remains available in the public domain.

III. Social and Economic Justice

9. **Eradicate poverty as an ethical, social, and environmental imperative.**

   a. Guarantee the right to potable water, clean air, food security, uncontaminated soil, shelter, and safe sanitation, allocating the national and international resources required.

   b. Empower every human being with the education and resources to secure a sustainable livelihood, and provide social security and safety nets for those who are unable to support themselves.

   c. Recognize the ignored, protect the vulnerable, serve those who suffer, and enable them to develop their capacities and to pursue their aspirations.

10. **Ensure that economic activities and institutions at all levels promote human development in an equitable and sustainable manner.**

   a. Promote the equitable distribution of wealth within nations and among nations.

   b. Enhance the intellectual, financial, technical, and social resources of developing nations, and relieve them of onerous international debt.

   c. Ensure that all trade supports sustainable resource use, environmental protection, and progressive labor standards.

   d. Require multinational corporations and international financial organizations to act transparently in the public good, and hold them accountable for the consequences of their activities.

11. **Affirm gender equality and equity as prerequisites to sustainable development and ensure universal access to education, health care, and economic opportunity.**

   a. Secure the human rights of women and girls and end all violence against them.

   b. Promote the active participation of women in all aspects of economic, political, civil, social, and cultural life as full and equal partners, decision makers, leaders, and beneficiaries.

   c. Strengthen families and ensure the safety and loving nurture of all family members.

12. **Uphold the right of all, without discrimination, to a natural and social environment supportive of human dignity, bodily health, and spiritual well-being, with special attention to the rights of indigenous peoples and minorities.**

a. Eliminate discrimination in all its forms, such as that based on race, color, sex, sexual orientation, religion, language, and national, ethnic or social origin.

b. Affirm the right of indigenous peoples to their spirituality, knowledge, lands and resources and to their related practice of sustainable livelihoods.

c. Honor and support the young people of our communities, enabling them to fulfill their essential role in creating sustainable societies.

d. Protect and restore outstanding places of cultural and spiritual significance.

IV. Democracy, Nonviolence, and Peace

13. **Strengthen democratic institutions at all levels, and provide transparency and accountability in governance, inclusive participation in decision making, and access to justice.**

a. Uphold the right of everyone to receive clear and timely information on environmental matters and all development plans and activities which are likely to affect them or in which they have an interest.

b. Support local, regional and global civil society, and promote the meaningful participation of all interested individuals and organizations in decision making.

c. Protect the rights to freedom of opinion, expression, peaceful assembly, association, and dissent.

d. Institute effective and efficient access to administrative and independent judicial procedures, including remedies and redress for environmental harm and the threat of such harm.

e. Eliminate corruption in all public and private institutions.

f. Strengthen local communities, enabling them to care for their environments, and assign environmental responsibilities to the levels of government where they can be carried out most effectively.

14. **Integrate into formal education and life-long learning the knowledge, values, and skills needed for a sustainable way of life.**

a. Provide all, especially children and youth, with educational opportunities that empower them to contribute actively to sustainable development.

b. Promote the contribution of the arts and humanities as well as the sciences in sustainability education.

c. Enhance the role of the mass media in raising awareness of ecological and social challenges.

d. Recognize the importance of moral and spiritual education for sustainable living.

15. **Treat all living beings with respect and consideration.**

a. Prevent cruelty to animals kept in human societies and protect them from suffering.

b. Protect wild animals from methods of hunting, trapping, and fishing that cause extreme, prolonged, or avoidable suffering.

c. Avoid or eliminate to the full extent possible the taking or destruction of non-targeted species.

16. **Promote a culture of tolerance, nonviolence, and peace.**

a. Encourage and support mutual understanding, solidarity, and cooperation among all peoples and within and among nations.

b. Implement comprehensive strategies to prevent violent conflict and use collaborative problem solving to manage and resolve environmental conflicts and other disputes.

c. Demilitarize national security systems to the level of a non-provocative defense posture, and convert military resources to peaceful purposes, including ecological restoration.

d. Eliminate nuclear, biological, and toxic weapons and other weapons of mass destruction.

e. Ensure that the use of orbital and outer space supports environmental protection and peace.

f. Recognize that peace is the wholeness created by right relationships with oneself, other persons, other cultures, other life, Earth, and the larger whole of which all are a part.

THE WAY FORWARD

As never before in history, common destiny beckons us to seek a new beginning. Such renewal is the promise of these Earth Charter principles. To fulfill this promise, we must commit ourselves to adopt and promoté the values and objectives of the Charter.

This requires a change of mind and heart. It requires a new sense of global interdependence and universal responsibility. We must imaginatively develop and apply the vision of a sustainable way of life locally, nationally, regionally, and globally. Our cultural diversity is a precious heritage and different cultures will find their own distinctive ways to realize the vision. We must deepen and expand the global dialogue that generated the Earth Charter, for we have much to learn from the ongoing collaborative search for truth and wisdom.

Life often involves tensions between important values. This can mean difficult choices. However, we must find ways to harmonize diversity with unity, the exercise of freedom with the common good, short-term objectives with long-term goals. Every individual, family, organization, and community has a vital role to play. The arts, sciences, religions, educational institutions, media, businesses, nongovernmental organizations, and governments are all called to offer creative leadership. The partnership of government, civil society, and business is essential for effective governance.

In order to build a sustainable global community, the nations of the world must renew their commitment to the United Nations, fulfill their obligations under existing international agreements, and support the implementation of Earth Charter principles with an international legally binding instrument on environment and development.

Let ours be a time remembered for the awakening of a new reverence for life, the firm resolve to achieve sustainability, the quickening of the struggle for justice and peace, and the joyful celebration of life.

For more information please contact:
Mirian Vilela, Executive Director
Earth Charter International Secretariat
c/o University for Peace
P. O. Box 138-6100 San José, Costa Rica
Phone: (506) 205-9060
Fax: (506) 249-1929
Email: info@Earthcharter.org
Website: www.Earthcharter.org

Appendix B

A COVENANT

FOR HONORING CHILDREN

BY RAFFI CAVOUKIAN

We find these joys to be self evident: That all children are created whole, endowed with innate intelligence, with dignity and wonder, worthy of respect. The embodiment of life, liberty and happiness, children are original blessings, here to learn their own song. Every girl and boy is entitled to love, to dream and belong to a loving "village." And to pursue a life of purpose.

We affirm our duty to nourish and nurture the young, to honour their caring ideals as the heart of being human. To recognize the early years as the foundation of life, and to cherish the contribution of young children to human evolution.

We commit ourselves to peaceful ways and vow to keep from harm or neglect these, our most vulnerable citizens. As guardians of their prosperity we honour the bountiful Earth whose diversity sustains us. Thus we pledge our love for generations to come.

CHILD HONOURING PRINCIPLES

The words of *A Covenant for Honoring Children* suggest nine guiding principles for living. Taken together, they offer a holistic way of restoring natural and human communities, thus brightening the outlook for the world we share. They form the basis for a multi-faith consensus on societal renewal.

RESPECTFUL LOVE

is key. It speaks to the need to respect children as whole people and to encourage them to know their own voices. Children need the kind of love that sees them as legitimate beings, persons in their own right. Respectful love instils self-worth; it's the prime nutrient in human development. Children need this not only from parents and caregivers, but from the whole community.

DIVERSITY

is about abundance: of human dreams, intelligences, cultures, and cosmologies; of Earthly splendours and ecosystems. Introducing children to biodiversity and human diversity at an early age builds on their innate curiosity. There's a world of natural wonders to discover, and a wealth of cultures, of ways to be human. Comforted by how much we share, we're able to delight in our differences.

CARING COMMUNITY

refers to the "village" it takes to raise a child. The community can positively affect the lives of its children. Child-friendly shopkeepers, family resource centres, green schoolyards, bicycle lanes, and pesticide-free parks are some of the ways a community can support its young.

CONSCIOUS PARENTING

can be taught from an early age; it begins with empathy for newborns. Elementary and secondary schools could teach nurturant parenting (neither permissive nor oppressive) and provide insight into the child-rearing process. Such knowledge helps to deter teen pregnancies and unwanted children. Emotionally aware parents are much less likely to perpetuate abuse or neglect.

EMOTIONAL INTELLIGENCE

sums up what early life is about: a time for exploring emotions in a safe setting, learning about feelings and how to express them. Those who feel loved are most able to learn and to show compassion for others. Emotional management builds character and is more important to later success than IQ. Cooperation, play, and creativity all foster the "EQ" needed for a joyful life.

NONVIOLENCE

is central to emotional maturity, to family relations, to community values, and to the character of societies that aspire to live in peace. It means more than the absence of aggression; it means living with compassion. Regarding children, it means no corporal punishment, no humiliation, no coercion. "First do no harm," the physicians' oath, must now apply to all our relations; it can become a mantra for our times. A culture of peace begins in a nonviolent heart, and a loving home.

SAFE ENVIRONMENTS

foster a child's feeling of security and belonging. The very young need protection from the toxic influences that permeate modern life – from domestic neglect and maltreatment, to the corporate manipulations of their minds, to the poisonous chemicals entering their bodies. The first years are when children are most impressionable and vulnerable; they need safeguarding.

SUSTAINABILITY

refers not merely to conservation of resources, renewable energy development, and anti-pollution laws. To be sustainable, societies need to build social capacity by investing in their young citizens, harnessing the productive power of a contented heart. The loving potential of every young child is a potent source for good in the world.

ETHICAL COMMERCE

is fundamental to a child-honouring world. It includes a revolution in the design, manufacture and sale of goods; corporate reform; "triple bottom line" business; full-cost accounting; tax and subsidy shifts; political and economic cycles that reward long-term thinking. Ethical commerce would enable a restorative economy devoted to the well being of the very young.

Appendix C

Renewing the Sacred Balance

Dinner Speech Delivered by Very Reverend Bill Phipps
Korlly's Restaurant
Sponsored by the Islamic Foundation Centre
Scarborough, Ontario
January 25, 2005

It is wonderful to be here with so many people of Canada's rainbow of faith traditions. This is a unique event, and part of a growing global consciousness that the planetary home we share is very sick, and desperately needs our collective attention. I believe that our presence tonight indicates that, deep in our hearts, we know the Earth cries out for our tender love.

I am overjoyed at the leadership given by so many people for the event tonight. It is not easy to organize an event such as this. I'm sure there were glitches along the way, but these pale in the light of the significance of what we are doing here.

Thank you to the Islamic Foundation of Toronto, to Ahmed; to the providers of this wonderful meal we have enjoyed; to Ted Reeve and Katharine Vansittart of Faith and the Common Good; and to the many people whose names I do not know. Thank you to David Suzuki for prevailing in his travels from the snowbound Maritimes.

Faith and the Common Good began about four years ago with the conviction that the public issues of the common good that Canada faces require a response, and action, from the voices of all our faith traditions. We believe that many issues of the common good are spiritual issues, as well as being economic or political issues. We believe that the social ethics of our various traditions have much in common, and that, therefore, we can stand on common ground for the common good. We are grateful for funding from the Atkinson and McConnell Foundations, from the Toronto School of Theology, and from other groups and individuals who share these convictions.

We began with a television program called *The Conscious Consumer.* In it, Jewish, Muslim, Buddhist and Ba'hai families discuss how they make economic/consumer decisions based on their faith. We followed this with another television program on health care, with a similar mix of faiths. This program was shown in 18 cities prior to the hearings on health care in Canada conducted by Roy Romanow.

For the last two years we have focused on *Renewing the Sacred Balance,* promoting David Suzuki's Nature Challenge in communities across Canada, from New Brunswick to Vancouver. This gathering tonight is a major event in this effort to engage faith traditions in the joyous celebration of sharing our sacred Earth.

Last Sunday was World Religion Day. In Ottawa, the multifaith community held a public event called "Many Faiths Sharing One Earth." All of our traditions share some common understandings and beliefs about the sacred gift of Earth. Reverence for, and the disease, health, and care *of* the Earth, is a spiritual matter of the deepest importance. The time is now for the faith traditions of the world to stand together and with one voice shout, "Stop the plunder now; come, join us in healing and caring for our only planetary home!"

I quote from the *Sourcebook of the World's Religions*[1]:

The healing of creation will not be accomplished by the judicious application of technology alone, but by a commitment that must be as intense as any religious faith. Our personal commitment to spiritual growth will lead us to ecologically responsible behaviour, because it will make clear the interrelatedness of all beings.

In fact caring for creation is a commitment for which the religions of the world provide the essential teachings. Faced with unprecedented global environmental and social crises, the challenge to us all is to recover the meaning of those teachings for today, to renew our kinship with all creation, to restore the primacy of spiritual values and of communal and personal spiritual growth, and to rediscover the simple truth: that there is no separateness and therefore there can be no selfishness, and that compassion for all is the heart of understanding.

And to highlight the tradition of our hosts tonight, the Islamic Foundation for Ecology and Environmental Sciences states, "Allah entrusted humanity with the guardianship of the Earth. We have to fulfill that ancient trust now before it becomes too late."[2]

I have a dream. Every community in Canada, indeed the world, has faith communities scattered in their midst. My dream is that they all join hands, each contributing their special beauty and care for the Earth, and stand together for the common good of healing our sacred home.

What a vision: a network of hope, a network of spiritual power, a network of humanity living out their spiritual identity. Joined together for the love of this sacred Earth, envision a network of compassion exploring the Holy Mystery.

I believe that we are called into such a relationship for the sake of the Earth and for all that is good, beautiful, and sacred.

I am honoured to introduce David Suzuki: scientist, communicator, lover of life, and compassionate companion of all who care for our fragile planet. No one has communicated as clearly as he both the crisis and the opportunities before us regarding ecological integrity. Instead of listing his credentials, I want to tell a story of David, set in Calgary two months ago.

A group of young teens have been working through Faith and the Common Good and Renewing the Sacred Balance. When they heard that David was coming to town to launch his latest and truly wonderful book, *Tree*, they were first in line for the event. He is their hero. At the end of David's talk there was a "Question and Answer" period. One of these young people asked David about the mess that his generation has been left with. Usually quick with excellent answers, David choked up. He paused and in a quavering voice remarked, "We haven't done a very good job, have we?" These words were from a man who devotes every waking hour to healing the planet.

He speaks from a tender heart and a passionate love. Ladies and gentlemen, David Suzuki.

---

[1] Joel Beversluis, ed., *Source Book of the World's Religions* (Novato, CA: New World Library, 2000).

[2] In an E-release, November/December 2002.

Appendix D

The United Church of Canada and the Apologies to First Nations Peoples

Delivered by The Right Reverend Robert Smith, Moderator of The United Church of Canada at Sudbury, Ontario, 1986.

Long before my people journeyed to this land your people were here, and you received from your elders an understanding of creation, and of the Mystery that surrounds us all, that was deep, and rich, and to be treasured.

We did not hear you when you shared your vision. In our zeal to tell you the good news of Jesus Christ we were closed to the value of your spirituality.

We confused Western ways and culture with the depth and breadth and length and height of the gospel of Christ.

We imposed our civilization as a condition of accepting the Gospel.

We tried to make you like us and in doing so we helped to destroy the vision that made you what you were. As a result, you, and we, are poorer and the image of the Creator in us is twisted, blurred, and we are not what we are meant by God to be.

We ask you to forgive us and to walk together with us in the spirit of Christ so that our peoples may be blessed and God's creation healed.

Delivered by Elder Edith Memnook, All Native Circle Conference representative at Victoria, British Columbia, 1988.

The Apology made to the Native Peoples of Canada by The United Church of Canada in Sudbury, in August 1986, has been a very important step forward. It is heartening to see that The United Church of Canada is a forerunner in making this Apology to Native Peoples. The All Native Circle Conference has now acknowledged your Apology. Our people have continued to affirm the teachings of the Native way of life. Our spiritual teachings and values have taught us to uphold the Sacred Fire, to be guardians of Mother Earth and to strive to maintain harmony and peaceful coexistence with all peoples.

We only ask of you to respect our Sacred Fire, the Creation, and to live in peaceful coexistence with us.

We recognize the hurts and feelings will continue amongst our peoples, but through partnership and walking hand in hand, the Indian spirit will eventually heal. Through our love, understanding, and sincerity the brotherhood and sisterhood of unity, strength and respect can be achieved.

The Native People of the All Native Circle Conference hope and pray that the Apology is not symbolic, but that these are the words of action and sincerity. We appreciate the freedom for culture and religious expression. In the new spirit the Apology has created, let us unite our hearts and minds in the wholeness of life that the Great Spirit has given us.

Delivered by The Right Reverend Bill Phipps, Moderator of The United Church of Canada at Toronto, Ontario, 1998.

I am here today as Moderator of The United Church of Canada to speak the words that many people have wanted to hear for a very long time. On behalf of The United Church of Canada, I apologize for the pain and suffering that our church's involvement in the Indian Residential School system has caused. We are aware of some of the damage that this cruel and ill-conceived system of assimilation has perpetrated on Canada's First Nations peoples. For this we are truly and most humbly sorry.

To those individuals who were physically, sexually, and mentally abused as students of the Indian Residential Schools in which The United Church of Canada was involved, I offer you our most sincere apology. You did nothing wrong. You were and are the victims of evil acts that cannot under any circumstances be justified or excused. We pray that you will hear the sincerity of our words today and that you will witness the living out of this apology in our actions in the future.

We know that many within our church will still not understand why each of us must bear the scar, the blame for this horrendous period in Canadian history. But the truth is we are the bearers of many blessings from our ancestors, and therefore we must also bear their burdens. We must now seek ways of healing ourselves, as well as our relationships with First Nations peoples. This apology is not an end in itself. We are in the midst of a long and painful journey. A journey that began with the United Church's Apology of 1986, to our Statement of Repentance in 1997, and now moving to this apology with regard to Indian Residential Schools. As Moderator of The United Church of Canada, I urge each and every member of the church to reflect on these issues and to join us as we travel this difficult road of repentance, reconciliation, and healing.

Appendix E

An *Ottawa Citizen* Q&A: Is Jesus God?

A conversation with United Church Moderator Rev. Bill Phipps

Editor's note: Our recent editorial board meeting with Rev. Bill Phipps, moderator of the United Church of Canada, sparked lively debate among readers. Following is an edited transcript of the conversation.

Rev. Phipps (in introductory remarks): People are yearning for a strong moral voice again in public policy. I think most people sense that we've lost our moral centre, that society has lost its moral centre. The United Church, over its 72-year history, has been one of the fairly strong moral voices, or strong social conscience, for Canada, and it has contributed a great deal over the years to the development of the Canada we once knew. So we've been a major player in the Canadian social fabric, social-moral-political-spiritual fabric.

But over the past 15 years, a lot of that, for a whole variety of reasons, has really diminished. We, along with a lot of the other churches, have gone from being mainline in terms of part of the moral centre to sideline. No one really cares or no one is really aware of what the church says.

The Citizen: How do we recover the moral centre? Political activism, that sort of thing?

Rev. Phipps: My evidence for where I think it's gone are things like language. I have now been transformed from a student to a consumer of education, a consumer of health care, a consumer of social services. Our language over the past 10 or 15 years has almost been single-mindedly changed into a market-economy language. I think the only value of – the primary value that we seem to have adopted in the past 10 or 15 years – is the market. Let the market decide. The market, the bottom line, profit and loss, winners and losers, have been the language of not only economic debate but all the other debates that go on.

If you express concerns about poverty and start using language that expresses compassion and solidarity with victims of social policy and so on, you're more accused now of being either wishy-washy or a bleeding heart or you don't understand the realities of the world, you don't understand that we are in a global death struggle with global competition and so on. It used to be that you could bring the values of compassion and empathy and solidarity to the table, and most people would say those are values we've got to listen to. My sense is that people listen to profit, loss and market. So it's not just political activism, it's where the conversations take place that have to do with the development of social policy...

Jesus talks about economics more than he talks about anything else. But what happens in experience is that moral questions get reduced to: I don't beat my kids, I get along with the public, the PTA, I don't have sex out of marriage and blah-blah-blah... Some of the giants of Canadian commerce were Methodists who were absolutely moral, upstanding people in their churches but paid low wages to their workers and adamantly opposed unions.

The Citizen: I can't help but notice that the emblem you are wearing is not a religious, but a political one (editor's note: the emblem was a lapel button reading "Zero poverty"). I would have expected a cross on the lapel of the moderator of the United Church. You haven't mentioned Jesus. Now, the Promise Keepers said that the critical thing is not whether you beat your dog or have extramarital sex; the critical thing, the foundation of everything, the centre of how you work is your relationship with Jesus, and it seems to me that a person who had a proper relationship with Jesus, who had opened his heart to believe in Jesus, would not engage in actions that harmed other people near or far.

Rev. Phipps: The experience has been otherwise. And I'm sorry the experience has been otherwise, but one of the worst regimes outside of the Nazi regime of this century has been the apartheid regime in South Africa, which was justified on biblical grounds by high-minded Christians, mainly men. The whole system of apartheid was put in place by high-minded Christian individuals who had no problem putting in place what we now know, and what a lot of us fought against for a long time: a totally obscene, unbiblical, unjust, I mean all the words you want, system of exploitation of people. But it was put in place with all the Christian rhetoric by Christian individuals who love Jesus.

The Citizen: Nevertheless, should the United Church parishioners not have a true relationship with Jesus?

Rev. Phipps: I think that goes on in every one of our 4,000 congregations every Sunday. I know it goes on where I'm the preacher and where I lead prayer; we have three Bible studies in the congregation of Calgary. A congregation of 180 adults comes to worship on Sunday morning, we have three Bible studies every week, we have a Eucharist and prayer service every Wednesday morning at 10 minutes after 7 to pray for members of the congregation who are in trouble.

In fact, I think, in many respects, another thing that's happened as we've kind of withdrawn a bit from the public world, the United Church has recovered a great deal of its biblical study and spirituality and its personal understanding of the faith, personal relationships with God and so on. That's going on far more than it did in the Church where I grew up as a kid. I've always been in the United Church, I'm 55 and I think there's far more serious biblical study going on, serious prayer groups and spiritual development. People never went on retreats. Geez, now we're going on retreats more than the Catholics are. You know? We're going to Catholic retreat centres. We keep them in business in some places.

So I think the United Church and other churches as well are doing a much better job than we ever did of that personal thing, and what I'm saying is we've never forgotten the focus, but we've got to be far more active and alive and let people know what we think about certain issues.

The Citizen: Unless you believe in Jesus, you will not be saved. Do you believe that?

Rev. Phipps: That Jesus is the only way to God?

The Citizen: Yes.

Rev. Phipps: No I do not believe that.

The Citizen: Do you believe that Jesus rose from the dead?

Rev. Phipps: I believe Jesus lives in people's hearts and did from the moment of that Easter experience.

The Citizen: But did he die, spend three days dead and rise from the dead and walk the Earth?

Rev. Phipps: No, I don't believe that in terms of the scientific fact. I don't know whether those things happened or not. Actually, I'm far more open to strange things happening and all that kind of thing than I used to be. I think it's an irrelevant question.

The Citizen: So, if Christ be not risen, our faith is in vain.

Rev. Phipps: No. No, no. Christ risen in people's hearts is extremely important. Something extraordinary happened that hadn't happened before in biblical records of resurrection to those people after they experienced Jesus alive. Obviously something absolutely stupendous happened to turn a bunch of cowards into people who are willing to lay down their own life.

But I wasn't there. But I'm the recipient to people who had a passion that Jesus was alive and well and not only in my heart but cruising around the world, trying to mend a broken world…

The Citizen: But the gospel is reported as literally being fact.

Rev. Phipps: Well, the gospels were written by people with a theological axe to grind and an agenda and fine, that's what they are. But they weren't historical records of anything.

The Citizen: Do you believe that Jesus is divine, that he was the son of God?

Rev. Phipps: We could have a whole discussion about that.

The Citizen: Well, I would think the head of a Christian church would have a clearly defined position on the issue. You have a clearly defined position on this world, but I'm asking about theology. What interests me about theology – and afterlife is more important to me than a soup kitchen.

Rev. Phipps: It wasn't to Jesus and it wasn't to people of the Bible… Your soul is directly tied (to) whether you care about people who are starving in the streets. Your soul is lost unless you care about that. In a country as wealthy as Canada… there is absolutely no excuse, speaking as a Christian, for there to be any soup kitchens, anybody living in the streets of Calgary, any shelters for the homeless. There should be no excuse for that in a place as wealthy as Calgary and a place as wealthy as Canada, biblically.

The Citizen: "The poor you will always have with you." That seems…

Rev. Phipps: No, unless you read the rest of that passage in Deuteronomy. People just like to lift it out and say there it is, Jesus said it. Read the whole Deuteronomy passage. If you have a Bible, we'll read it.

Soul has to do with those very practical social justice issues. It always has in scripture and it certainly did with Jesus. That's why I said Jesus talked a lot more about economics than he did about anything else.

The Citizen: In this argument, morality has become quite situational and is subject to fashion, and I'm wondering how you respond to that.

Rev. Phipps: Well, I think that's absolutely true, but those are two different things. "Subject to fashion" I think is absolutely right. What is the morality of the day? But you'd have to be more specific about that. Morality and ethics always has to relate to the situation in which you're in. I'm one of those people who's very wary about people who write down a bunch of rules and say that is going to pertain forever and ever. You look at some of morality and there's no way we'd follow those examples now. The main example is slavery and women. Those were just accepted parts of the social structure. It was not immoral

to treat women as property. Well, it certainly is immoral to do that now.

The Citizen: Then what is the moral centre? If it's situational, then certainly there's no centre.

Rev. Phipps: The centre is in biblical terms, our concepts or words or experiences as compassion, justice, peace. The Jewish term "shalom" encompasses a whole lot of things. Peace with justice. There is no peace where there is no justice. It's how you apply that in a given situation. People, Christian people as part of the apartheid system, thought that peace with justice was there. Then people come along, like Bishop Tutu, say "Wait a minute, your concept of justice and peace is wrong. We don't have peace and justice."

The Citizen: I certainly see that in the situation of apartheid, but if morality is situational, who's to say that the people who come after apartheid are therefore correct?

Rev. Phipps: I could put that in the whole doctrine of original sin. Maybe a good example of this is our relationship with native people. In 1986, the United Church made an apology to native people for taking away their language, their religion, their culture and so on in the name of Christ. Our Methodist forebears and so on came over to convert the heathens to Christianity. I would never condemn them. They believed they were exercising their Christianity, and if you read some of their stuff, you're appalled at the language and so on.

But alongside those comments are comments of love and concern, and sacrifice to be with those native people. My white ancestors sacrificed a lot, a lot more than I ever sacrificed, to do what they thought their Christian duty called them to do.

Now in retrospect we say much of what they did was wrong. Now I know that much of what I do people are going to look back in 50 or 100 years and say, "Gee, you know, they were misguided on free trade," maybe. Or on some other things that we believe in. That's because we're sinful people. We see through the glass darkly and we do our very best where we can. I don't have a problem with situationalism or those kinds of things. But I constantly have to ask myself: What is just? It clearly to me is unjust in a wealthy place like Canada that there are any poor people at all. Biblically, it's totally an abomination.

The Citizen: That's an absolute, then. You said you were uncomfortable with absolute rules, thou shalt not kill, thou shalt –

Rev. Phipps: Not absolute rules. In my context, in 1997, in the relative affluence of Canada, it is an obscenity that the gap between rich an poor is widening even more.

The Citizen: So would it not be an obscenity anywhere, in a society that is affluent?

Rev. Phipps: Probably.

The Citizen: So that's an absolute. It doesn't depend on circumstance. "No peace without justice." That's a moral absolute, isn't it? You're not that uncomfortable with moral absolutes, provided that you agree with them.

Rev. Phipps: No, no. I – those are terms that describe – if you want to call that a moral absolute. But how does that work out? What does love work out to be? In my grandparents' time, people living together without benefit of marriage was totally immoral. They were very strong Methodists in the United Church. And probably – and it wouldn't matter if they loved each other and were committed to each other – if they hadn't gone through a marriage ceremony, then that was immoral. Having a child out of wedlock was immoral and we hid them away, and that's how we did it. And I think now that it's not necessarily immoral to live with somebody without benefit of marriage.

Well, what does love mean? Well, if you're committed and you're not promiscuous and genuine love and mutual love and respect, then the act of marriage is not necessary for that relationship to be a moral, loving just relationship. Now that's changed in just two generations.

The Citizen: A true change or just a perception of it?

Rev. Phipps: The truth is love. The criterion is love, not a marriage certificate. I know you can write the moderator of the United Church of Canada does not believe in marriage, and that's not true. I believe very strongly in marriage. I'm a divorced person and I have remarried. Now we could just as easily have lived together. But we said no, we want to have this public ceremony of a recognition of our love and all that.

The Citizen: Why call it holy matrimony? Why say: "What God has joined together let no man pull asunder"? If getting married is not a commitment to God, how does it have any moral significance?

Rev. Phipps: Well, I think God and Jesus were a good example of this. Whether Jesus is God or represents God. Jesus' many questions were a question of love, not the trappings of it. And on that particular thing, I'm sure God would say: "Who cares if it's a Christian marriage or not?" These people loved each other in a committed relationship, raised a family, looked after them. That's what God is concerned about. How we treat each other. What our relationships are like. Are they relationships of loving justice or, too often, you know, we cover up lack of love with elaborate social paraphernalia...

I believe that Christ reveals to us as much of the nature of God as we can see in a human being. Now that has some presuppositions to it, the major one of which is that life and death and God, the Divine and the Holy and all that, is a tremendous mystery of which anyone sees only a very small part. There is all kinds of stuff to discover that we don't know about. But as far as we are able to understand, Christ is that person who reveals to us the most about the nature of God, what God wants of us, who God is, of any human being.

The Citizen: So was Christ God?

Rev. Phipps: No, I don't believe Christ was God.

The Citizen: He's not part of the Trinity. He's not the son of God.

Rev. Phipps: I think that's – I'm no theologian.

The Citizen: You're the head of a Christian church, you have to be.

Rev. Phipps: No, I don't have to. I'm no theologian, but the beauty of the Trinity to me is that it recognizes various dimensions to the Christian understanding of God. If Jesus was God, there'd be no need for God in the Trinity.

The Citizen: I guess what I'm trying to get at is, is there any truth that the United Church, or Bill Phipps, agrees with? Is there any truth that we can say: "You believe in this. This is what the United Church says, this is what the moderator says, whatever…"

Rev. Phipps: The fundamental truth to me in the biblical story is that God loves us and the world unconditionally, and part of that unconditional love is, for Christians, it was that unconditional love was poured into the person of Jesus. The whole biblical story is one of God's unconditional love. Taking people who betrayed God, who said no to God, who were unjust and converting them and turning them around. Moses would be one example, that's a huge truth as far as I'm concerned, because a lot of people want to have a conditional love of God.

Part of the whole implication, to me, of the truth of God's unconditional love for the world is the freedom to try and bring justice and fail. The ethical outgrowth of God's unconditional love is just relationships in the Earth among human communities. If God loves me and everybody unconditionally, it means I can try to act justly, I can be vigorous in my engagement with the world, and fail. And God will love me. That's a pretty strong statement.

The Citizen: Is there a heaven?

Rev. Phipps: Is there a heaven, a place? I have no idea. I believe there is.

The Citizen: Do we all join with God in the afterlife regardless of our conduct? Does anyone get shut out? Some people get the gate in the face?

Rev. Phipps: I have no idea. But I just want to say something about unconditional love, seeing God as a loving parent. Anyone who has children knows what it is to love your child unconditionally and have heartache about your child. But we know – that's what unconditional love is.

The story of the prodigal son is one of the great stories about that and there are other stories and many religious traditions.

The Citizen: What's the worst thing that could happen to me when I die?

Rev. Phipps: The worst thing that could happen to you is that your worst fears of Dante's Inferno are actually true, that's the worst thing that could happen to you.

The Citizen: So there actually is a hell? And it's very bad?

Rev. Phipps: I have no idea. And I don't think Jesus was that concerned about hell. I think we're concerned about life here. And the Jewish tradition wasn't that concerned about hell either. They were concerned about just relationships here. I've got enough problems, and I think most of us have enough problems, trying to live an ethical life knowing all of the ways we compromise ourselves and all of the frailties that we've got. We've got enough problems trying to live ethically and well here to have any knowledge or understanding or worry about what happens after I die.

I believe there is a continuation of the spirit in some form or another, but I'd be a fool to say I know what that is or what it's going to be like.

The Citizen: But does it exist? When Jesus said –

Rev. Phipps: I think there is a continuation of spirit in some way or another, but I have no idea how it is.

Responses from the Moderator

November 01, 1997: Moderator's Reply to Criticism

The following is taken from Note 428 by CONF BC on Oct. 30, 1997 at 14:55 Eastern (4185 characters) and is a copy of a News Release from General Council Offices wherein the Moderator responds to the criticism occasioned by his interview with the Ottawa Citizen.

A Statement by the Moderator, The Right Reverend Bill Phipps, in response to discussion following the article in the *Ottawa Citizen* on Friday, October 24, 1997.

Over the last few days there has been both negative and positive reactions to a story in the *Ottawa Citizen* resulting from a one and three quarter hour interview with me by their Editorial Board. With one or two minor exceptions I think Bob Harvey did a good job of summarizing what was a long, open, and free ranging discussion.

I did not expect the grilling I received on Christian orthodoxy, but I did not shrink from any of their questions. It was clear that the opinions expressed by me were mine alone and, unless stated specifically, not United Church policy. However, I believe that nothing I said is outside the broad mainstream of United Church belief. I believe my faith is well rooted in scripture and Christian tradition, although it is not frozen in the language of early creeds for example.

My beliefs were born and nurtured in a strong United Church family, conservative in thought, theology, politics, and behaviour. While still influenced by that loving environment, through study and experience my faith has grown, deepened and changed. As a pastor I never wish to hurt anyone, and I always respect the faith, experience, and convictions of other people. As a church leader, I hope I am able to challenge all of us in the understanding of our faith and its relevance to our changing and stress-filled society. I believe passionately that the God we know in Christ Jesus is as compelling for us as he was 2000 years ago in inviting people into deep spiritual experience and active critique of the principalities and powers which engulf and enslave the world.

I believe that in Jesus we know as much of God as is possible in a human being, but he did not reveal nor represent all of God. The God of the Bible is never completely known nor understood, yet is as intimate and compassionate as the most loving parent. I have experienced the presence of God at my mother's death bed and in the streets of New York City. In response to "what does God require of us?" (Micah 6:8) Jesus continues to call his followers to "do justice, love tenderly, and walk humbly with God."

There is no question that the followers of Jesus experienced God's transforming power in the resurrection. Jesus was so alive for them that they were driven to risking their lives in proclaiming the Gospel. The "resurrection event" is difficult to harmonize in the Gospel accounts, but there is no doubt that Jesus becomes a living, transforming power in the lives of his followers, and continues to do so to this day.

I believe the current interest in the person of Jesus (as expressed in the Jesus Seminar, as one of many examples) is indicative of deep spiritual yearning in our society. I believe there is nothing to fear in open, honest, and informed debate among us about these and other faith issues. Indeed, the strength of our United Church is its acceptance of wide ranging viewpoints and encouragement of the lively exchange of ideas.

Thank God that the general public is also interested in a credible expression of Christian faith in our cynical age. And thank God that we are rooted in a tradition which welcomes discussion, discovery, and transformation. May we debate vigorously with one another while always respecting each other as human beings, creatures of a God whose love is unconditional.

I hope that the interest in the *Ottawa Citizen* article will be translated into study of "Reconciling and Making New: Who is Jesus for the world today?" This is an excellent study document authorized by the General Council, prepared by the national Theology and Faith Committee and mailed to every pastoral charge in May 1997.

A Personal Response to Letters and Emails to the Moderator

DATED DECEMBER 29, 1997

Dear Friends,

This generic letter is in response to the hundreds of pieces of correspondence I have received over the last eight weeks, triggered by my interview with the Editorial Board of the *Ottawa Citizen*. I regret that I am unable, at this time, to answer each letter individually and am only able to acknowledge your letter with this more general comment.

First of all, I do thank you for taking the time to write and express your opinion, whether positive or negative. Some of your letters were quick notes of support or disagreement. Other letters were detailed testimonies to your own understanding of the Christian faith and points at which you would agree or disagree with my remarks as reported in the press. For this, I thank all of you.

Attached to this letter you will find my initial statement clarifying my comments in the *Ottawa Citizen*. Although much more could be said, at least this gives a short clarification of my beliefs expressed over a long interview with them. It also invites the Church into a study of "Reconciling & Making New: Who is Jesus for the world today?" the United Church study on Christology available in each pastoral charge.

I grew up in a home and a United Church which valued honest differences of opinion, as well as learning from each other during the course of our faith journey. The correspondence I have received from you reveals a wide range of viewpoints about the nature of Scripture, the Creeds, and the revelation of God in Jesus Christ. I must say, however, that amongst the wide range of opinions there is unanimity about the importance of God's revelation in Jesus and the centrality of the Scriptures in understanding our faith. We must also remember that the United Church is rooted in the various articulations of the Christian faith from the early Creeds to the most recent version of the United Church Creed formulated in 1968.

I am also impressed with the depth of faith you expressed from wherever you stand along the theological continuum. I believe our United Church is strong and well-placed to engage in faithful and vigorous discussion about faith in our personal lives and for the relevance of the Gospel of Jesus Christ for the brokenness of the world in which we live.

There is no question that there are thousands of Canadians talking about Jesus and religious matters who otherwise would not dream of doing such a thing. My hope is that we will support and challenge each other as we continue to seek faithfulness in following the way of Jesus. In all the correspondence which I have received, I have been privileged to hear some marvellous stories of faith questions being opened up in new and fresh ways, and stories of peoples' own journey which leads them into ever-stronger convictions.

To those who disagree with some of the things I have said, I thank you for being forthright and clear as to where you stand. It takes courage to write and to express views in clear terms and I appreciate you taking the time to make your views known. I have read all the letters and have given them all careful consideration. I also want you to know that I honour the place where you stand within the range of Christian tradition, and faithfulness.

To those who have agreed with much of what I have said, I thank you for your encouragement and support. Some of your stories have been overwhelming in their joy and hope for the future of our Church and our place in the world. So thank you for taking the time to write, and to encourage me in my role of Moderator.

Thank you for sharing this part of your life with me. May we continue to honour each other's testimonies of faith while living our own convictions as prayerfully as possible.

Peace,

Rt. Rev. Bill Phipps, Moderator
The United Church of Canada

Bibliography

Armstrong, Karen. *A History of God*. New York: Alfred Knopf, 1993.

Asch, Michael, and Norman Zlothin, eds. *Aboriginal and Treaty Rights in Canada*. 1997.

Astigas, Mariano. *The Mind of the Universe: Understanding Science and Religion*. Philadelphia: Templeton Foundation Press, 2000.

Axworthy, Lloyd. *Navigating a New World: Canada's Global Future*. New York: Alfred Knopf, 2003.

Bakan, Joel. *The Corporation*. Toronto: Viking Canada, 2004.

Barlow, Maude, and Tony Clarke. *Blue Gold: The Battle Against Corporate Theft of the World's Water*. Toronto: Soddart, 2002.

Bateman, Robert. *Thinking Like a Mountain*. Toronto: Viking, 2000.

Berry, Thomas. *The Great Work: Our Way into the Future*. New York: Bell Tower, 1999.

—. *The Dream of the Earth*. San Francisco: Sierra Club Books, 1988.

Berry, Wendell. *Life is a Miracle: An Essay Against Modern Superstition*. Washington, D. C.: Counterpoint, 2000.

Boff, Leonardo. *Cry of the Earth, Cry of the Poor*. Maryknoll, NY: Orbis, 1997.

Borg, Marcus. *The Heart of Christianity: Rediscovering a Life of Faith*. San Francisco: HarperSanFrancisco, 2003.

Breton, Mary Joy. *Women Pioneers for the Environment*. Boston: Northeastern University Press, 1998.

Brower, David, and Steve Chapple. *Let the Mountains Talk, Let the Rivers Run*. New York: Harper Collins, 1995.

Brown, Lester. *Eco-Economy*. New York: W. W. Norton, 2001.

Brueggemann, Walter. *The Prophetic Imagination*. Minneapolis: Augsburg Fortress Press, 1978.

—. *Hope for the World*. Louisville, KY: Westminster John Knox Press, 2001.

—. *The Hopeful Imagination*. Minneapolis: Augsburg Fortress Press, 1986.

Capra, Fritjof. *The Hidden Connections: A Science for Sustainable Living*. New York: Anchor Books, 2004.

Carr, David. *Earth in Mind*. Washington: Island Press, 1994.

Cavanagh, John and Jerry Mander, eds. *Alternatives to Economic Globalization*. San Francisco: Berrett –Koehler, 2004.

Cavoukian, Raffi and Sharna Olfman, eds. *Child Honoring: How to Turn this World Around*. Westport, CT: Praeger, 2006.

Chamberlain, Edward. *If This Is Your Land, Where Are Your Stories?: Reimaging Home and Sacred Space*. Cleveland: The Pilgrim Press, 2004.

Conlon, James. *At the Edge of Our Longing*. Ottawa: Novalis, 2004.

Dallaire, Romeo. *Shake Hands with the Devil*. Toronto: Random House, 2003.

De Villiers, Marq. *Water*. Toronto: Stoddart, 1999.

Del Re, Guiseppe. *The Cosmic Dance: Science Discovers the Mysterious Harmony of the Universe*. Philadelphia: Templeton Foundation Press, 2000.

Diamond, Jared. *Collapse*. New York: Viking, 2005.

Ditmars, Hadani. *Dancing in the No-Fly Zone: A Woman's Journey through Iraq*. Vancouver: Raincoast Books, 2005.

Drohan, Madelaine. *Making a Killing: How and Why Corporations Use Armed Force to Do Business*. New York: Random House, 2003.

Eisler, Riane. *The Chalice and the Blade*. San Francisco: Harper and Row, 1988.

—. *The Power of Partnership*. Novato, CA: New World Library, 2002.

Eldredge, Niles. *Life in the Balance: Humanity and the Biodiversity Crisis*. Princeton, NJ: Princeton University Press, 1998.

Emoto, Masau. *The Hidden Message in Water*. Hillsboro, OR: Beyond Words Publishing, 2004.

Fawcett, Brian. *Virtual Clearcut or The Way Things Are in My Hometown*. Toronto: Thomas Allen, 2003.

Flannery, Tim. *The Weather Makers*. New York: Harper Collins, 2005.

Fox, Matthew. *A New Reformation*. Rochester: Inner Traditions, 2006.

—. *The Coming of the Cosmic Christ*. San Francisco: HarperSanFrancisco, 1988.

Glavin, Terry. *Waiting for the Macaws*. Toronto: Viking, 2006.

Greene, Brian. *The Elegant Universe*. New York: W.W. Norton, 1999.

Grey, Mary. *Sacred Longings: Ecological Spirit and Global Culture*. Minneapolis: Augsburg Fortress Press, 2004.

Hall, Douglas John. *Confessing the Faith*. Minneapolis: Augsburg Fortress Press, 1996.

—. *Professing the Faith*. Minneapolis: Augsburg Fortress Press, 1993.

—. *The Cross in Our Context*. Minneapolis: Augsburg Fortress Press, 2003.

—. *Thinking the Faith*. Minneapolis: Augsburg Fortress Press, 1989.

—. *Why Christianity?* Minneapolis: Augsburg Fortress Press, 1998.

Hallman, David, ed. *Ecotheology: Voices from South and North*. Mayknoll, NY: Orbis Books, 1994.

—. *Spiritual Values for Earth Community*. Rick Series, World Council of Churches, 2000.

Hanh, Thich Nhat. *No Death, No Fear*. New York: Riverhead Books, 2002.

—. *Peace is Every Step*. New York: Bantam, 1992.

Hartmann, Thom. *The Last Hours of Ancient Sunlight*. New York: Three Rivers Press, 1998, 2004.

Harvey, Andrew. *Son of Man: The Mystical Path to Christ*. New York: Torcher/Putnam, 1998.

Paul Hawken. *Blessed Unrest: How the Largest Movement in the World Came into Being and Why No One Saw It Coming*. New York: Viking, 2007.

—. *The Ecology of Commerce*. New York: Harper Collins, 1993.

Hawken, Paul, Amory Lovins, and L. Hunter Lovins. *Natural Capitalism: Creating the Next Industrial Revolution*. New York: Little Brown, 1999.

Hayden, Tom. *The Last Gospel of the Earth*. San Francisco: Sierra Club Books, 1996.

Hedges, Chris. *American Fascists: The Christian Right and the War on America*. New York: Free Press, Simon and Shuster, 2006.

Helliwell, John F. *Globalization and Well-Being*. Vancouver: University of British Columbia Press, 2002.

Herzog, Kristin. *Children and Our Global Future*. Cleveland: The Pilgrim Press, 2005.

Hessel, Dieter and Rosemary Radford Reuther. *Christianity and Ecology*. Boston: Centre for World Religions, Harvard University Press, 1999.

Hessel, Dieter, and Larry Rasmussen, eds. *Earth Habitat*. Minneapolis: Augsburg Fortress Press, 2001.

Homer-Dixon, Thomas. *The Upside of Down: Catastrophe, Creativity and the Renewal of Civilization*. Toronto: Alfred Knopf, 2006.

Hutton, Will and Anthony Giddens, eds. *Global Capitalism*. New York: The New Press, 2000.

Jackson, Wes. *Becoming Native to this Place*. Lexington, KY: University Press of Kentucky, 1994.

Jacobs, Jane. *Dark Age Ahead*. New York: Random House, 2004.

Kaitter, Paul. *One Earth Many Religions: Multifaith Dialogue and Global Responsibility*. Maryknoll, NJ: Orbis, 1985.

Kingsolver, Barbara. *Small Wonder: Essays*. New York: HarperCollins, 2002.

Korten, David C. *The Post-Corporate World: Life after Capitalism*. San Francisco: Berrett-Koehler, 2000.

—. *The Great Turning: From Empire to Earth Community*. San Francisco: Berrett-Koehler, 2006.

—. *When Corporations Rule the World*. San Francisco: Berrett-Koehler, 1995.

Kunstler, James H. *The Long Emergency: Surviving the End of Oil, Climate Change, and Other Converging Catastrophes of the Twenty-First Century.* Atlantic Monthly Press, 2005.

Leakey, Richard, and Roger Lewin. *The Sixth Extinction: Patterns of Life and the Future of Humankind.* London: Weidenfeld and Nicolson, 1996.

Leeming, David. *Myth: A Biography of Belief.* New York: Oxford University Press, 2002.

Lessing, Doris. *Mara and Dann.* London: Flamingo (HarperCollins), 1999.

Levine, Stephen. *A Year to Live: How to Live This Year as If It Was Your Last.* New York: Harmony/Bell Tower, 1997.

Lopez, Barry. *Arctic Dreams.* New York: Bantam Books, 1988.

Mander, Jerry, and Edward Goldsmith, eds. *The Case Against the Global Economy.* San Francisco: Sierra Club Books, 1996.

—. *In the Absence of the Sacred.* San Francisco: Sierra Club Books, 1991.

Marmur, Dow. *Six Lives: A Memoir.* Toronto: Key Porter, 2004.

May, Elizabeth. *At the Cutting Edge.* Toronto: Key Porter, 2005.

McDaniel, Carl. *Wisdom for a Livable Planet.* San Antonio, TX: Trinity University Press, 2005.

McFague, Sallie. *The Body of God: An Ecological Theology.* Minneapolis: Augsburg Fortress Press, 1993.

McKibben, Bill. *Deep Economy: The Wealth of Communities and the Durable Future.* New York: Times Books/Henry Holt and Company, 2007.

Melnyk, George, ed. *Canada and the New American Empire.* Calgary, AB: University of Calgary Press, 2004.

Michell, Alanna. *Dancing at the Dead Sea.* Toronto: Key Porter, 2004.

Mistry, Rohinton. *A Fine Balance.* Toronto: McClelland and Stewart, 1995.

Moe-Lobeda, Cynthia. *Healing a Broken World: Globalization and God.* Minneapolis: Augsburg Fortress Press, 2002.

Monbiot, George. *Heat: How to Stop the Planet from Burning.* Toronto: Doubleday, 2006.

Muller, Wayne. *Sabbath.* New York: Bantam Books, 1999.

Ó Murchu, Diarmuid. *Evolutionary Faith: Rediscovering God in Our Great Story.* Maryknoll, NY: Orbis Books, 2004.

—. *Reclaiming Spirituality.* New York: Crossroad Publishing, 2000.

Pogue, Carolyn. *A New Day: Peacemaking Stories and Activities.* Toronto: United Church Press, 2005.

Raffan, James. *Tumblehome: Meditations and Lore from a Canoesist's Life.* Toronto: HarperCollins, 2001.

Reuther, Rosemary Radford. *Women Health Earth: Third World Women on Ecology, Feminism and Religion.* Maryknoll, NY: Orbis Books, 1996.

Rowe, Stan. *Earth Alive: Essays on Ecology.* Vancouver: New West Press, 2006.

Sachs, Jeffrey. *The End of Poverty.* New York: Penguin Press, 2005.

Sanguin, Bruce. *Darwin, Divinity, and the Dance of the Cosmos: An Ecological Christianity.* Kelowna, BC: CopperHouse/Wood Lake Publishing, 2007.

Scharper, Stephen Bede. *Redeeming the Time: A Political Theology of the Environment.* New York: Continuum, 1998.

Schwartzentruber, Michael, ed. *The Emerging Christian Way: Thoughts, Stories, and Wisdom for a Faith of Transformation.* Kelowna, BC: CopperHouse/Wood Lake Publishing, 2006.

Shiva, Vandana. *Water Wars: Privatization, Pollution and Profit.* Toronto: Between the Lines, 2002.

—. *Biopiracy: The Plunder of Nature and Knowledge.* Boston: South End Press, 1997.

Soyinka, Wole, *Climate of Fear: The Quest for Dignity in a Dehumanized Word.* New York: Random House, 2005.

Stannard, Russell, ed. *God for the Twenty-first Century.* Philadelphia: Templeton Foundation Press, 2000.

Stone, Michael K., and Zenobia Barlow. *Ecological Literacy: Educating Our Children for a Sustainable World.* San Francisco: Sierra Club Books, 2005.

Suzuki, David, and Holly Dressel. *Good News for a Change: Hope for a Troubled Planet.* Toronto: Stoddart, 2002.

—. *From Naked Ape to Superspecies.* Toronto: Stoddart, 1999.

Suzuki, David, and Amanda McConnell. *The Sacred Balance: Rediscovering our Place in Nature.* Vancouver: Greystone, 2002.

Swimme, Brian. *The Hidden Heart of the Cosmos: Humanity and the New Story.* Maryknoll, NY: Orbis Books, 1996.

Tucker, Mary Evelyn. *Worldly Wonder: Religions Enter Their Ecological Phase.* Chicago: Open Court, 2003.

Turner, Nancy J. *The Earth's Blanket: Traditional Teachings for Sustainable Living.* Vancouver: Douglas and McIntyre, 2005.

Vaillant, John. *The Golden Spruce.* Toronto: Vintage Canada, 2005.

Vanier, Jean. *Becoming Human.* Toronto: Anansi Press, 1998.

Wallis, Jim. *God's Politics: Why the Right Gets It Wrong and the Left Doesn't Get It.* San Francisco: HarperSanFrancisco, 2005.

Wink, Walter. *The Powers That Be.* New York: Doubleday, 1998.

Wright, Ronald. *A Scientific Romance.* Redding Ridge, CT: Black Swan Books, 2002.

—. *A Short History of Progress.* Toronto: Anansi Press, 2004.

Magazines and Newspapers

Alberta Views	*Harpers*	*The United Church Observer*
Briar Patch	*Resurgence*	*The Walrus*
Canadian Dimension	*The CCPA Monitor*	*Tikkun*
Guardian Weekly	*The Parkland Post*	*Yes!*

The Very Reverend Dr. BILL PHIPPS serves on the Consortium for Peace Studies at the University of Calgary and is co-founder of the Faith and the Common Good network. He served as Moderator of the United Church of Canada from 1997 to 2000.

Bill has had a varied career as lawyer, community organizer, hospital chaplain, adult educator, and minister. He holds academic degrees from the University of Toronto, Osgoode Hall Law School, and McCormick Theological Seminary in Chicago; as well as honorary degrees from Victoria University in the University of Toronto, and St. Stephen's College, Edmonton.

Bill is married to writer Carolyn Pogue, author of *After the Beginning, A World of Faith,* and many other books for youth on peace.